"I often talk to people who feel 'living insanity' defines them more than 'living in sanity.' But one doesn't move from the former to the latter without intention and a plan. *Crafting a Rule of Life* offers a practical and doable process to move your life from insanely busy and driven to the sweet sanity of ordered work and rest. Biblical and historical guides accompany you on the crafting journey. Steve's book is a wonderful tool for your journey."

ADELE CALHOUN, author of *Spiritual Disciplines Handbook* and *Invitations from God*

"*Crafting a Rule of Life* is a special gift of grace for all who seek a more faithful and fulfilling way of living as a follower of Jesus Christ. Steve Macchia clearly and compellingly writes about the value of a disciplined way of living for individuals and small groups, and then offers a carefully constructed pathway to find that more faithful and fulfilling way."

RUEBEN P. JOB, coauthor of *A Guide to Prayer for Ministers and Other Servants* and retired bishop of the United Methodist Church

"Whether our lives are overregulated or disheveled, a 'rule of life' may be what we need—and this book will help. It is not about 'rules' but about the end and purpose of life—to know and love God and become all he made us to be. Read it as a guide to shaping a life, neither frittered away in self-indulgence nor constrained by expectations of others, but growing into the fullness of Christ. You will find Steve Macchia to be a wise and seasoned companion on the way."

LEIGHTON FORD, author of *The Attentive Life*

"Helping people develop their own personal rule of life so that their lives truly revolve around the love of Jesus is one of the most important issues facing the church today. Steve has made a wonderful contribution in writing this practical, thorough book. I highly recommend it!"

PETE SCAZZERO, pastor and author of *Emotionally Healthy Spirituality*

"In *Crafting a Rule of Life* Steve Macchia tackles the central question facing the intentional disciple of Jesus Christ: How do I shape the rhythms of my life so I can walk with God? Steve's gentle, wise and practical guidance will help you draw closer to Jesus on a day-by-day basis. This is not a book to miss."

CHRISTOPHER WEBB, president of Renovaré USA and author of *The Fire of the Word*

STEPHEN A. MACCHIA

FOREWORD BY MARK BUCHANAN

❖

CRAFTING A
RULE OF LIFE

An Invitation to

the Well-Ordered Way

IVP Books

An imprint of InterVarsity Press
Downers Grove, Illinois

InterVarsity Press
P.O. Box 1400, Downers Grove, IL 60515-1426
World Wide Web: www.ivpress.com
E-mail: email@ivpress.com

InterVarsity Press® is the book-publishing division of InterVarsity Christian Fellowship/USA®, a movement of students and faculty active on campus at hundreds of universities, colleges and schools of nursing in the United States of America, and a member movement of the International Fellowship of Evangelical Students. For information about local and regional activities, write Public Relations Dept., InterVarsity Christian Fellowship/USA, 6400 Schroeder Rd., P.O. Box 7895, Madison, WI 53707-7895, or visit the IVCF website at <www.intervarsity.org>.

While all stories in this book are true, some names and identifying information in this book have been changed to protect the privacy of the individuals involved.

Cover design: Cindy Kiple
Interior design: Beth Hagenberg
Images: ©Geoff Eley/Trevillion Images

ISBN 978-0-8308-3564-5

Printed in the United States of America ∞

Library of Congress Cataloging-in-Publication Data

Macchia, Stephen A., 1956-
  Crafting a rule of life: an invitation to the well-ordered way /
Stephen A. Macchia.
     p. cm.
  Includes bibliographical references (p.   )
  ISBN 978-0-8308-3564-5 (pbk.: alk. paper)
  1. Benedict, Saint, Abbot of Monte Cassino. Regula. 2. Spiritual
life—Christianity. 3. Christian life. I. Title.
  BX3004.Z5M25 2012
  248.4—dc23

                                                                    2011047308

P	23	22	21	20	19	18	17	16	15	14	13	12	11	10	9	8	7	6	5	4	3	2	1
Y	31	30	29	28	27	26	25	24	23	22	21	20	19	18	17	16	15	14	13	12			

*This book is dedicated to the many relationships that have
created, redeemed, sustained and transformed the life God has
invited me to humbly fulfill for his glory:*

My dearly loved family, Ruth, Nathan and Rebekah

Leadership Transformations, Inc., board of directors and ministry team

Gordon-Conwell Theological Seminary Pierce Center staff team and fellows

*Beloved mentors, colleagues, extended family and friends, sisters and
brothers in Christ who continue to pour life into my soul and
companion me on the path of life*

CONTENTS

———❖———

You have made known to me the path of life;

you will fill me with joy in your presence,

with eternal pleasures at your right hand.

Psalm 16:11

FOREWORD

This past week, as part of my pastoral rounds, I visited two women in their eighties. Both were in separate hospitals. I saw Elly on Monday and Elizabeth on Thursday. The first was a planned visit—Elly has been in extended care for several months, growing ever more brittle-boned, wispy-voiced, crepe-skinned, not long for this world. The second was unscheduled—Elizabeth took a tumble while doing her own daily rounds of visits to the weak and the ailing. She broke her hip and was awaiting emergency surgery. She lay in the hospital bed, quite cheerful on morphine, her bluish hair impeccably neat, and looked her usual sweet, formidable self. I'd give her another twenty years before she's off to the wild blue yonder.

Both are living saints. They are women of deep goodness and fierce prayer and holy mischief. Elly, only a few years ago, wrote her autobiography. It's called *Counting My Blessings*, which she's spent a lifetime doing. We spent our visit counting more. She is a kind of abacus of thanksgiving in flesh and blood.

Elizabeth never misses an opportunity to tell anyone in earshot about the love of God. I know she'll use her forced bed confinement for this: to her, it's just a brilliant ploy of divine providence to place her in arms' reach of a whole phalanx of hospital patients and medical staff. By the time she's discharged, a small village will have heard the good news of great joy. I think the apostle Paul would have trouble keeping up with her.

I pay these kind of visits often enough. I have the privilege of brushing up against people like this every week. It's as if I have a hall pass to wander the gallery of saints in Hebrews 11. What gave these visits added poignancy was the book you're now holding, Steve Macchia's *Crafting a Rule of Life*, which I was in the midst of reading. One of the many virtues of this book is how gloriously free it is from mere theorizing and armchair speculation. Indeed, Steve earths every lesson in real life, his own and others', including brilliant vignettes of historical personages to illustrate the spiritual values he discusses in each chapter.

He could have used Elly and Elizabeth.

Which is exactly the point. Steve, in these pages, has lovingly rendered a tremendous service to the church. He unfolds the deep-down stuff that lies beneath the lives of people like that. Spiritual robustness like theirs, so tenacious and subversive and attractive, doesn't happen by accident. It doesn't happen overnight. It doesn't happen by wishing or trying.

It is a long obedience in the same direction. It is forged in the daily and tempered in the ordinary. It is a slow and steady and deliberate gathering of the years. It is a combination of keen attentiveness—to God, to self, to others, to life—and holy indifference—to trifles, to insults, to useless distractions. It is planned, not in some goose-stepping mechanical way, but in the sense that it builds on a resolve to take hold of that for which Christ Jesus took hold of you, and to take every though captive and make it obedient to Christ.

Most of us stumble into the kingdom with nary a clue how to do this. So we thrash about, make reckless attempts, arm ourselves with slogans, goad ourselves with guilt, fail and fail and fail, and finally settle for spiritual mediocrity. Our inner lives remain cramped and musty. We resort to mere conformity, to a masquerade of piety to cover up for our lack of real Christlikeness. And when we meet an Elly or an Elizabeth, they fill us with wistfulness or shame or cynicism.

Herein lies another option: to craft a rule of life which perfectly fits your unique temperament, bent, background and passion, and which day by day, week by week, month by month, year by year, decade by decade, makes God real to you in the inmost places. That's what this book will help you do, gently, clearly, persuasively, comprehensively.

The genius of Steve's approach is he makes ancient ways contemporary, personal and practical. Saint Benedict joins your daily commute. St. Augustine goes to the gym with you. George Mueller helps you reconcile your bank statement. There's no need to live in a cave or meditate atop a pillar. The life you long to live can be fashioned from the life you already have. You just need someone like Steve to show you how.

I read this book fast to write this foreword. Now I'll read it again, slow, to heed its counsel. Lucky you: you're free to get right down to business.

Happy crafting, living saint.

Mark Buchanan
Author of *The Rest of God* and *Your Church Is Too Safe*
Blog: www.markbuchanan.net

INTRODUCTION

Crafting a Personal Rule of Life

Take your everyday, ordinary life—your sleeping, eating, going-to-work, and walking-around life—and place it before God as an offering. Embracing what God does for you is the best thing you can do for him. Don't become so well-adjusted to your culture that you fit into it without even thinking. Instead, fix your attention on God. You'll be changed from the inside out. Readily recognize what he wants from you, and quickly respond to it. Unlike the culture around you, always dragging you down to its level of immaturity, God brings the best out of you, develops well-formed maturity in you.

ROMANS 12:1-2 *THE MESSAGE*

Fix your attention on God and you'll be changed from the inside out. God is the one who brings out the best of you. That's a truth worth pursuing with our whole hearts. God lovingly invites us to pursue our shared calling as a Christian community *and* our unique vocation as individual disciples. There is only one Moses, one Ruth, one Peter, one James, one John—and only one you.

We are all on a common pursuit of loving God, loving one another and loving others in Jesus' name. We do so in slightly different ways—reflected in the tens of thousands of denominational niches worldwide—but more importantly, we call ourselves Christian and mean it from the bottom of our hearts. Our commonality is a beautiful gift to reflect on and is our delightful inheritance. We are set apart and called to be the people of God, "a chosen people, a royal priesthood, a holy nation, a people belonging to God, that we may declare the praises of him who called you out of darkness into his wonderful light" (1 Peter 2:9). But even though we all live our lives in a wider community, we also find ourselves in daily pursuit of a life that's uniquely set apart for God's distinct purposes—evidenced in our personal rule of life.

What Is a Personal Rule of Life?

Your personal rule of life is a holistic description of the Spirit-empowered rhythms and relationships that create, redeem, sustain and transform the life God invites you to humbly fulfill for Christ's glory.

What do you think of when you hear the word "rule"? For many of us, the word has negative connotations. We are likely to think of rules as boundaries that *forbid* us from doing something. But a rule of life is something else. Rather than being a set of laws that forbid us to do certain things, a rule of life is a set of guidelines that *support* or *enable* us to do the things we want and need to do.

A rule of life allows us to clarify our deepest values, our most important relationships, our most authentic hopes and dreams, our most meaningful work, our highest priorities. It allows us to live with intention and purpose in the present moment.

The word "rule" derives from a Latin word, *regula,* which implies not so much a system of rules or laws, but rather a way of regulating or regularizing our lives so that we can stay on the path we have set out for ourselves. A rule is like a trellis which offers support and guidance for a plant, helping it to grow in a certain direction. A rule of life is *descriptive* in that it articulates our intentions and identifies the ways in which we want to live. And when we fall short of these intentions, the rule becomes *prescriptive*, showing us how we can return to the path that we have set for ourselves and recapture our original vision. It is not something fixed and rigid, but something which can and should be adapted to our present circumstances and shaped to fit our current needs and desires.

In the ancient sense of the term, *regula* or rule meant "guidepost" or "railing," something to hang on to in the dark, that leads in a given direction, points out the road or gives us support as we climb. It's created of the raw material of our lives and it assumes no great wisdom or spiritual depth to understand. Instead, it's an invitation to life in all its fullness, depending on God and listening attentively to his voice. And it's fulfilled in the simple routines of everyday life, bursting forth from a well-ordered heart and resulting in the well-ordered way.

All of us have an unwritten personal rule of life that we are following, some with great clarity, others unknowingly. We wake at certain times, get ready for our days in particular ways, use our free time for assorted purposes and practice rhythms of work, hobbies, worship, vacation and so on. There is already a rule in place that you are following today. Isn't it time to give up our unwritten rule and prayerfully write one that more closely matches the heartbeat of God?

Those who fail to do so are like wild, untamed grape vines. They will produce some fruit, but they probably won't be as abundant as they could be. Instead, they become more vulnerable to things that threaten their spiritual vitality. However, those who are intentionally reflective, prayerful and attentively responsive are like cultivated vines. Growing on a trellis (a rule of life) and cultivated toward maturity, they become spiritually formed. The trellis curbs our tendency to wander and supports our rather frail attempts to be nurtured spiritually. Our lives will produce an abundance of fruit for the glory of God. Mature vines are cultivated to produce the best fruit.

Though your life seems full, does it at times feel unfulfilling and empty? Perhaps you may be allowing others to define how you should live. Do you yearn to hear the voice of God louder than that of a parent, family member, friend, teacher, pastor, boss or leader? Do you feel the need for clarity and focus? Or are you looking for a way out of boredom and mediocrity? Perhaps you long for a refreshing, renewing lifestyle. Whatever the reason or life situation, you feel compelled to consider the invitation God has for you today. He is calling you to himself, gifting you for service and empowering you for the abundant life.

Benedict: A Life of Listening

Many centuries ago, one hero of the faith chose purposefully to live the Christian faith counterculturally. Around A.D. 540, Benedict developed a rule of life for faithful followers of Christ. In the midst of increasing religious and secular pressures, Benedict began the journey of discerning the will of God for himself and those he lived with.

In his classic "Little Rule for Beginners" Benedict's opening word is *Listen!* He offers a way of listening in a safe, faith-filled community environment. Here God's voice can be heard by those seeking him through humility and obedience. In community, like-minded and like-hearted believers best learn to practice the disciplines of prayer, healthy relationships and good works.

According to Benedict, God becomes the primary informant of the heart and mind when believers learn to listen to his voice. Out of this posture of listening, God calls each one to loving intimacy in prayer, faith and life. Such a disciplined journey may be difficult at first, Benedict confesses, but "as we progress in this life and in faith, our hearts will expand with the inexpressible joy of love as we run the way of God's commandments." Thus the ultimate outcome of living by a rule of life is joy. Loving worship and faith-filled service to God produces pure joy. This is the pathway to the abundance of life.

Born to privilege in the tiny hill village of Nursia (now known as Norcia), Italy, Benedict was raised in a wealthy Roman home, where he was taught that family is the most sacred institution, with the father as its most respected leader. The other guiding principle was that one must be obedient to a worthy communal cause. Both principles—family and community—ultimately shaped his rule. Nevertheless, Benedict had to make some radical decisions regarding how to live.

His first radical decision was to leave this privileged life to become a student of rhetoric in Rome. But Benedict soon discovered he had little in common with his classmates, who preferred the cycle of studying and drunken partying. So he left the academy and pursued a countercultural life, ending up in a cave near the Anio River in Subiaco, Italy. Here, in a narrow, ten-foot-deep cave, Benedict began his robust, deliberate, God-centered life. In this cave Benedict, with God's help, sorted out what it means to live the Christian life in a pagan world.

Benedict thought and prayed about how best to live for God in this world. His classic rule was crafted in isolation, but tested and transformed in community. In the cave Benedict came to the full realization that God's call was toward humility, as expressed both in contemplation (a life of prayer) and community (a life of love). This twofold priority became the backbone of Benedict's rule of life.

Following Benedict

Listening and *humility* are essential to the creation and fulfillment of our personal rule of life today. Rather than waiting on God to inform our hearts and direct our steps, we prefer following our own ideas about how to live. But without a humble, attentive heart, our self-centeredness will not lead to the abundance of a God-empowered life.

To discover your own personal rule of life takes time and concerted effort; you must listen to God and discern what he wants you to be and do for his glory. Fulfilling a personal rule of life, centered in the pursuit of a well-developed spiritual life within a predominantly secular society, is difficult to say the least. But it's certainly not impossible. The basic disciplines of Scripture, prayer and reflection will lead us forward in our journey toward Christlikeness. Discernment is central to crafting our rule of life.

Prayerfully set a course for the days ahead, asking God to shine a light on your spiritual rhythms and personal relationships. Do so in the reality of your daily life, anticipating your way forward into renewal, redemption and the abundance of life in Christ. Developing a personal rule of life grows out of a listening posture of humility and prayer. It awaits your diligent attentiveness every step of the way. Like a trellis for a wandering vine, your personal rule of life guides you intentionally forward, one section of the trellis at a time, until your whole life is encompassed.

A personal rule of life is a holistic description. Consider Adam and Eve (Genesis 2–3). Their God-inspired personal rule of life was to be lived out in a lush garden with one simple instruction: eat here and not there. Their vision and mission was clearly stated, the garden was ripe for its cultivation, the relationships were ideal, and the only requirement was to listen and obey. The enemy of our soul wants to pull us off the trellis to wander and fend for ourselves. Like Adam and Eve, our personal rule of life affects our whole life. And like them we too will fall short of God's intentions and need to daily realign our lives. When crafting your rule of life, consider the entirety of your life.

A personal rule of life is Spirit-empowered. Consider the early church (Acts 1–4). We see that their rule of life was freshly empowered by the experience of Pentecost and maintained in the unity of the Spirit. God's empowering presence is the first attribute of a healthy disciple, and is the key to understanding one's rule of life. When we trust God to grant us the fruit and the gifts of the Spirit and live by them, we learn what it means to live for the glory of God and the expansion of his kingdom. Our rule of life is best lived out under the guidance and empowerment of God's Spirit.

A personal rule of life includes both the rhythms and relationships of life. Consider Joseph (Genesis 37–50). Joseph was thrown into a pit by his jealous brothers, but he remained faithful, saying no to his tempter and even caring for his brothers, who betrayed him. Later, from a position of power and authority, he chose the preemptive attitude of forgiveness, grace and mercy. His religious *rhythms* and practices fostered an abundance of life for those around him. As a result, his life was redeemed, sustained and transformed for God's glory.

Consider Elizabeth, Zechariah, Mary, Joseph and even the shepherds (Luke 1–2). The first advent of Christ arrived in the midst of a small spiritual community of *relationships*. All were led by the Spirit, and each had a calling and mission to fulfill. Even though one person, Zechariah, was silenced in the process, each relationship was intertwined within this extended family. Each was expectant and hopeful, and without competition they encouraged one other toward the fulfillment of their unique vocation. When they realized they were created for a unique purpose, each life was redeemed, sustained and transformed for Christ. The first advent story was their greatest fulfillment and joy.

A personal rule of life is to be humbly fulfilled for Christ's glory. Consider the faithful characters in the biblical hall of faith (Hebrews 11). We see that there was no pride or self-absorption among the faithful. They lived for God's honor and glory, suffered on God's behalf, and watched how God used them for purposes that grew much larger than they could ever have asked, dreamed or imagined for themselves.

Jesus is the ideal example of the embodiment of a Spirit-empowered personal rule of life. Jesus' ability to balance attentiveness to the Father and to his daily life is scattered throughout the Gospels. His community of disciples, where loving accountability was the centerpiece, is a model to embrace. Jesus provides the example and the inspiration to move forward in developing intimacy with God out of which we discover our own personal rule of life. Jesus maintained that balanced posture of life and service to others. Likewise, our personal rule of life is to be holistic, covering each of the major areas of life. We also need to acknowledge that we, like Christ and the heroes of our faith in both the biblical text and throughout church history, are to see our personal rule of life as both countercultural (we march to the beat of a different drummer than the rest of the world) and counterintuitive (we live for Christ and therefore need to die to self and our own natural inclinations to always put self first).

Discovering your personal rule of life will encompass every aspect of your life in Christ. The invitation is transformational, so brace yourself for sweet release. By letting go and trusting God, you will receive the gift of life in its fullest and richest form.

How Will Each Chapter Unfold?

Since life is so complex and multifaceted, you will be guided through one main issue at a time as you build your rule of life. Each chapter will include the following features:

Guiding principle. Each guiding principle will shape the development of a personal rule of life in specific and personally meaningful ways. You will be given questions to prayerfully consider before further defining the principle at hand.

Biblical reflection. Through the introduction of biblical characters and the use of interactive Bible study, you will be invited to dig deeply into God's Word. As the story comes alive, you will begin to see with the renewed eyes of your heart how the biblical story informs the development of your personal story.

Historical insight. You will be welcomed into the challenging and inspirational stories of fascinating men and women of the church. Each will stimulate your thinking and prod your personal reflections on what makes for a faith-shaped life.

Personal rule of life. Questions and reflection exercises will help you to discern God's ongoing invitation to the well-ordered way. Here also you will begin to write your rule of life—a section at time. As you work through the process, you will sense an ever-deepening awareness of God's voice speaking into your heart. Anticipate his loving hand guiding you into the fullness of his call and will for your life.

Spiritual community. This book is designed for use in community, and in this section you will find discussion questions to help you process what you are learning with others.

Learning in a Spiritual Community

It will be most helpful if you read one chapter at a time, answer the questions in each section and share your process of discovery with a small group of spiritual friends. When we speak with others about our experience in Christ, it sharpens our attentiveness to the voice and will of the Father. Sharing our stories helps us clarify the intentions of our hearts toward the fulfillment of his divine will. A small circle of friends also reminds us of the presence, power and protection of the Holy Spirit. Confiding in one another instills a sense of hope for the future as children who are dearly loved by their Father.

There are several spiritual community options to consider:

Small group. Spend time with an existing spiritual formation small group (or with one started for this purpose) for a few months while each member reads this material and begins to craft their first draft of a personal rule of life. If you choose this option, consider spending 90 minutes together: 15 minutes for gathering hospitality, 15 minutes for prayer and biblical reflection, 45 minutes to discuss the section's questions, and 15 minutes for intercessory prayer for one another.

Accountability triad. In a mini-group of three friends, hold one another accountable for completing the reading, reflection exercises and drafting a personal rule of life. You could also talk through the chapters on a weekly basis following the small group format above.

One-on-one with a spiritual friend. You could meet on a weekly basis to review each chapter, or you could simply meet for accountability and prayer on a weekly or monthly basis.

One-on-one with a spiritual director or mentor. If you already have a relationship with a spiritual director or another mentoring relationship, invite this spiritual guide to listen attentively to you as you craft your personal rule of life.

For more resources as you navigate this book visit www.ruleoflife.com.

Invitation to the Journey

Cease the continual striving of a life of nonstop technology, noise and activity. Stop looking exclusively to others' ideas of how you are to live as a Christian. Instead, begin to listen to God with an attentive, reflective and discerning heart. In the context of your spiritual community, take the necessary time to discover afresh his invitation to the abundant life. This journey of personal discovery is sure to be life transforming for you and all whose path you gracefully cross.

What better time than *now* to embrace a deeper understanding of your personal rule of life?

As you begin this process, let me encourage you to pursue this prayerfully, one piece at a time. Like putting together a puzzle, we will start with the frame or border, and work toward the center. To honor the Lord and allow you to attend to his still, small voice every step of the way, prayerful discernment is essential. I invite you to pray:

Lord, I honor you today as the cornerstone of my life and the joy of my heart. I want to seek your mind on how best to understand your personal rule of life for me. So, as I turn each page, read all of the writings, meditate on your Word, sit reflectively and creatively with the exercises before me, I ask for you to guide, protect and multiply the work of my hands and the prayers of my heart. For the sake of your name, the expansion of your kingdom and the enrichment of my life in you, dear God—Father, Son and Holy Spirit. Amen.

PART ONE

Framing Your Personal Rule of Life

What matters supremely, therefore, is not, in the last analysis, the fact that I know God, but the larger fact which underlies it—the fact that he knows me. I am graven on the palms of his hands. I am never out of his mind. All my knowledge of him depends on his sustained initiative in knowing me. I know him, because he first knew me, and continues to know me. He knows me as a friend, one who loves me; and there is no moment when his eye is off me, or his attention distracted from me, and no moment, therefore, when his care falters. This is momentous knowledge. There is unspeakable comfort—the sort of comfort that energizes, be it said, not enervates—in knowing that God is constantly taking care of me in love, and watching over me for my good. There is tremendous relief in knowing that his love to me is utterly realistic, based at every point on prior knowledge of the worst about me, so that no discovery now can disillusion him about me.

J. I. PACKER, *KNOWING GOD*

1

ROLES

What Are My Primary Relationships?

Guiding Principle

Roles: **Your personal rule of life is discerned and framed within the context of your primary relationships and your spiritual community, and lived out in service to others.**

In his book *Sacred Companions* David Benner discusses five interrelated elements that appear in healthy spiritual friendships: love, honesty, intimacy, mutuality (offering reciprocal care) and accompaniment (taking an active interest in each other's journey). I would add another characteristic of healthy friendships—the willingness and desire to listen. With these characteristics in mind, if you were ranking your ability to develop and sustain healthy relationships, on a scale of 1 (low) and 5 (high), how would you fare? Why?

> *Lord, make me an instrument of your peace;*
> *where there is hatred, let me sow love;*
> *where there is injury, pardon:*
> *where there is doubt, faith;*
> *where there is despair, hope*
> *where there is darkness, light*
> *where there is sadness, joy*
> *O divine Master,*
> *grant that I may not so much seek to be*
>   *consoled as to console;*
> *to be understood, as to understand;*
> *to be loved, as to love;*
> *for it is in giving that we receive,*
> *it is in pardoning that we are pardoned,*
> *and it is in dying that we are born to*
>   *Eternal Life.*
> *Amen.*
> —ATTRIBUTED TO ST. FRANCIS OF ASSISI

If your closest friend were answering this question for you, how do you think he or she would rank your ability to develop and sustain healthy relationships? Why?

If confronted by someone you recently were in conflict with, what do you think *that person* would say about your ability to redeem and transform your relationships? Why?

Think of your closest friend and also of someone you most recently had a conflict with. Write out the prayer of your heart regarding the desire you have for the health of your primary earthly relationships—beginning with strengthening the relationship you have with your best friend, as well as resolving a conflict you are having with another.

Biblical Reflection

**Create in me a pure heart, O God, and renew
a steadfast spirit within me. (Psalm 51:10)**

When we consider the relationships that matter most to our development as individuals made in the image of God, it's vital that we consider them in terms of the roles we fulfill. Some of our relationships stand alone in a particular role. Some roles encompass multiple relationships. My role as father includes two relationships—with our son and with our daughter. My role as boss envelopes many members of our ministry team. Others may co-mingle and cross over into various roles. For example, your boss might also be a friend; your spouse may be your business partner; your cousin might also serve on the same nonprofit board with you; or your pastor may be your golf buddy.

Sharing one or two roles is pretty normal, but when our relationships cross over into three or more roles, it can get pretty complicated. For example, when

my boss is also my friend and becomes my confidante and counselor, it's tough to maintain appropriate boundaries, confidentiality and objectivity—especially if something comes up at work that needs to be confronted. Or if your pastor/golf partner invites you to serve on the board and you find yourself in disagreement with him, does the golf all of a sudden come to an end?

How many roles and relationships can we handle well? Some would insist that it's impossible to sustain more than five to seven major roles and stay balanced and healthy. I am inclined to agree.

One person in the Bible who had multiple roles, responsibilities and relationships is King David, the greatest and most important king of Israel. The majority of his story is found in the books of 1–2 Samuel, 1 Kings and 1 Chronicles. From his early life until his death, David was involved in a variety of roles and relationships. Try adding them up and you'll be overwhelmed with what we know about David's life (1040-970 B.C.). It's no wonder he had an occasional fall from his pedestal of greatness:

- Within his family of origin, David was the eighth of his *brothers* and youngest *son* of Jesse of Bethlehem.

- In the early period of his life David is mentioned as a *man after God's own heart*, a title he maintained as he kept the divine commandments (1 Samuel 13:14). As a *shepherd* boy he showed great courage in protecting the flock (1 Samuel 17:34-36). As a youth he was an outstanding *athlete* (1 Samuel 17:34-36).

- David was a fine *musician* who played the harp before the king (1 Samuel 16:14-23). He was a *poet* and *psalmist* of the finest caliber, writing some of the great masterpieces of spiritual literature; no other poetry has been so consistently used by the church through the centuries as the many psalms of David.

- David was intimate *friend* to Jonathan (1 Samuel 20), King Saul's son (for whom he served as *armor bearer*). He was a courageous *champion* of Israel and killed the giant Goliath, which resulted in a great victory for God's people (1 Samuel 17:25-53). This was just the beginning of his ability to lead military campaigns as a successful *general*.

- David was *husband* to several wives and concubines and *father* to many children—mostly sons and at least one daughter (2 Samuel 5:14-16; 9:11;

13:1-29; 1 Chronicles 3:1-9; 2 Chronicles 11:18).

- David is also known for his turbulent adult life and his fallenness and depraved humanity as an *adulterer*. In his darkest hours as king, David's lust for Bathsheba led to the death of her husband, Uriah, and the eventual death of the child born to David and Bathsheba (2 Samuel 11–12).

- David was a *repentant sinner* brought back into fellowship with the living God through the prophet Nathan; his prayer of Psalm 51 is an example for all generations.

- David was divinely chosen to succeed King Saul and quietly anointed by the prophet Samuel (1 Samuel 16:12-13) to serve as *king* over Israel. He is considered a genius and the greatest of all kings, displaying unusual military victories and enlargement of the kingdom (2 Samuel 8, 10), providing wisdom in the administration of government (2 Samuel 5:3), in the capturing of Jerusalem (the "City of David") and the establishment of the capital there (2 Samuel 5:7). He *anointed his son Solomon* to serve as his successor (1 Kings 1:11-39; 2:1-9).

- He is the most famous *ancestor of Christ*—Jesus is not called the Son of Abraham or the Son of Jacob, but the Messiah, Son of David.

King David was a complex man. His roles were many and varied. Some were overlapping and others were misused for unfortunate and destructive ends. Each had their own set of possibilities and tensions, and it's astounding to consider how effective this man of God was when his entire life is considered. His personal rule of life was indeed framed within the wealth of his myriad roles and relationships, essential for understanding the life he was invited by God to fulfill.

The elegant writing of Psalm 51 is in response to Nathan the prophet's confrontation and rebuke of David's adultery with Bathsheba. As recorded in 2 Samuel 11 and 12, David fell hard to the lustful temptations of his heart toward the bathing Bathsheba next door. He summoned her to his palace and they slept together, consummating a relationship that would be both immediately cursed and ultimately blessed. His subsequent sins of having Uriah the Hittite (Bathsheba's husband) killed on the front lines of battle, lying about and covering up his sin, continued to wreak havoc on his soul.

By the time Nathan arrives on the scene, David is filled with guilt. Nathan begins by telling David a simple story of injustice: "There were two men in a certain town, one rich and the other poor. The rich man had a very large number of sheep and cattle, but the poor man had nothing except one little ewe lamb he had bought. He raised it, and it grew up with him and his children. It shared his food, drank from his cup and even slept in his arms. It was like a daughter to him. Now a traveler came to the rich man, but the rich man refrained from taking one of his own sheep or cattle to prepare a meal for the traveler who had come to him. Instead, he took the ewe lamb that belonged to the poor man

and prepared it for the one who had come to him" (2 Samuel 12:1-4).

After hearing this story, David is outraged: "As surely as the LORD lives, the man who did this deserves to die" (2 Samuel 12:5). Nathan responds to David, "You are the man!" (v. 7) and then proceeds to remind David of all that the Lord, the God of Israel, had done to raise David up to become king over Israel. Reminding David of his true personhood and identity in God was the linchpin to his own embracing of that identity as a man, a king, an honorable child of God.

The brilliance of Psalm 51 is captured in David's willingness to finally come clean and admit his sinfulness and brokenness, his desperate need for God's grace, mercy and forgiveness. Out of that place of freedom, he openly confesses his wrongdoings before the Lord. The purity of his heart is brought to light, and his renewed sense of confidence is evident for all to see.

As you and I consider our own roles and relationships, we do so out of our brokenness and our need for God's amazing grace in all of our interactions with others. David is a wonderful example for us to prayerfully consider as we begin to craft our rule of life around the many people we come in contact with on a daily basis. Sit with Psalm 51 and receive these words as a reminder of how you too can pray about your life and relationships. May this psalm set you free to admit your brokenness, your longing for joyfulness and your leanings toward restored faithfulness in your service to others throughout your sphere of influence.

1. One of David's dearest friends was Jonathan. Read through the account of their friendship in 1 Samuel 18–20. Note that "Jonathan became one in spirit with David, and he loved him as himself. . . . And Jonathan made a covenant with David" (1 Samuel 18:1-4), and "Saul told his son Jonathan and all the attendants to kill David. But Jonathan was very fond of David and warned him . . . 'Be on your guard . . . go into hiding'" (1 Samuel 19:1-3), and "we have sworn friendship with each other in the name of the LORD" (1 Samuel 20:42). What does it mean to make a covenant of love with our friends?

   Who would you be willing to make such a commitment to?

2. By far one of David's greatest failures was lusting after Bathsheba, which ended in adultery (2 Samuel 11–12). While David's men were fighting the enemy, he was sleeping with the wife of one of his top commanders. As a result, his life was turned upside down. David sought to hide his sin by calling Uriah home from the battlefield, thinking he would return to the arms and bed of Bathsheba. But Uriah refused. So David had him killed on the front lines of battle. After being confronted by Nathan the prophet, David finally admitted to his sin. Read Psalm 51, and as you reflect on this psalm, make it a prayer of your own. Jot down any relationships that possibly could be repaired if you sought forgiveness, mercy and reconciliation. What is the Lord inviting you to consider in this regard?

3. 1 Kings 2:1-3 recounts:

   > When the time drew near for David to die, he gave a charge to Solomon his son. "I am about to go the way of all the earth," he said. "So be strong, show yourself a man, and observe what the LORD your God requires: Walk in his ways, and keep his decrees and commands, his laws and requirements, as written in the Law of Moses, so that you may prosper in all you do and wherever you go."

   Consider one of your key roles and primary relationships. If given the opportunity, what words of blessing would you like to speak to that person? Jot down some ideas here and then prayerfully consider sharing them the next time you are together. You may want to repeat this exercise with other roles and relationships in mind.

Historical Insight

In the history of the church we find many notables who fulfilled several key roles and maintained a variety of relationships throughout their lives. One such prominent Christian leader is C. S. Lewis, a man who seized numerous roles in life including *novelist, academic, literary critic, lay theologian* and *apologist*. He is most widely known for his literary prowess (he wrote more than thirty books); his most celebrated works are The Chronicles of Narnia, *The Screwtape Letters* and *Mere Christianity*. He was by far one of the most intelligent and influential Christian writers of his day.

However, many of his readers do not know his personal story. In brief, Clive Staples Lewis (1898-1963) was born in Belfast, Ireland. He was known early in life as "Jack"—a nickname he gave to himself at the age of four after the beloved neighborhood dog "Jacksie" died. Lewis had one brother, Warren, and his mother, Florence, died of cancer when he was merely nine years old.

Lewis studied at Campbell College in Belfast and then Malvern College, where at the age of fifteen he became an atheist, abandoning his Christian upbringing in the Church of Ireland. He went on to study at Oxford, but took a hiatus from his studies after the outbreak of World War I, when he enlisted in the British Army. During his time in the army he became close friends with Paddy Moore, who was killed in battle. While serving together, Lewis promised that he would take care of Paddy's family if he died in battle. He was eventually discharged after he was wounded in the Battle of Arras. Lewis then followed through on his promise to his friend Paddy and looked after his mother and sister. Eventually, the three of them, along with Lewis's brother, Warren, moved into "The Kilns," where they all lived together for several years.

During Lewis's days teaching at Oxford, he went from being an atheist to a deeply committed Christian. He was converted to Christ in 1931. At that time he became a member of the Church of England and developed a profound understanding of the Christian faith. He attributes his coming back to Christianity to his friendship with J. R. R. Tolkien and the writings of G. K. Chesterton. His conversion had a profound effect on his work. His wartime BBC radio broadcasts on the subject of Christianity, which would later comprise the contents of his *Mere Christianity*, brought him wide acclaim. It was also during this season that Lewis became the central figure in the now famous literary group The Inklings. This group of friends met twice-weekly and included influential writers such as Tolkien, Hugo Dyson, Charles Williams and Robert Havard.

At fifty-eight Lewis married Joy Davidman Gresham, an American writer who was fifteen years his junior. Their marriage only lasted four years, when Joy died of bone cancer in 1960. Lewis thereafter cared for her two sons, Douglas and David Gresham. Lewis was devoted to Joy, and his writings about her loss in *A Grief Observed* are evidence of their profound love. He died three years later at his home, one week before his sixty-fifth birthday on November 22, 1963, the same day U.S. president John F. Kennedy was assassinated.

C. S. Lewis's roles were many and varied: influential and intellectual *writer* and *theologian*, deeply committed *friend*, *war hero*, *son*, *brother*, *husband*, *stepfather* and *spiritual father* to many others. In addition to these more obvious roles, Lewis was also a *spiritual director*. What's fascinating, however, is that his role as spiritual director was fulfilled primarily through the ministry of letter writing. He faithfully utilized the written medium, which made him so famous, in serving the spiritual needs of others.

Father Walter Adams, both an Anglican parish minister and a mission priest with the Society of Saint John the Evan-

gelist, was Lewis's spiritual mentor, confessor and father in Christ. Lewis met almost weekly with Adams for more than a decade. Through this relationship Lewis grew to love the Scriptures, evangelism, a passion for holiness, an appreciation of the writings of the early church fathers and a deep desire to really know the Lord Jesus Christ. "May it be the real I who speaks (in prayer)" and "may it be the real Thou that I speak to," Lewis wrote in *Letters to Malcolm*.

From the spiritual direction Lewis received from Adams, he obediently served others as their personal spiritual mentor—all through written letters. "C. S. Lewis in fact became—and still is—a spiritual guide of such high caliber that it rivals his stature as a Christian apologist." As Lewis's spiritual director would often remind him, "Look after the roots and the fruits will look after themselves." Lewis practiced this himself and helped many others as well. And this came from his commitment to the obedience required in following Christ, "I cannot learn to love my neighbor as myself until I learn to love God: and I cannot learn to love God except by learning to obey Him."

> Lewis' ability to treat each letter writer with dignity, his unflagging skill at honest encouragement and affirmation even when it must have been difficult, plus his skill at identifying with his correspondents through admission of his own flaws, all conspired to make him an effective soul caregiver. Equally impor-

tant, however, was his straight talk and tough love. There was no space in his letters for cheap grace. He insisted that discipleship is costly. Obedience is required. Forgiveness covers all who truly repent, and Bible truth needs to be confronted.

Using Christ-centered words, Lewis's ministry of spiritual direction was profound. From this vantage point he encouraged others toward peace, holiness and eternal life. Lewis promoted as staples for a healthy spiritual diet the disciplines of confession, repentance, prayer and the Bible.

C. S. Lewis was a man of many roles and relationships. He fulfilled his roles with integrity, depth, faithfulness and serious resolve. His inspirational life is a model to study and learn from today.

Personal Rule of Life

1. List all your key relationships (names) and the role you play in each (father or mother, brother or sister, boss, colleague, student, friend). It's fine to list multiple roles next to more in-depth or complex relationships.

2. Place a qualitative number (1, relatively unhealthy, to 5, relatively healthy) next to each key relationship. Include helpful and descriptive commentary. Who might need to hear from you a word of encouragement and/or affirmation, of apology and/or reconciliation?

3. Place a "+" sign next to the roles that are most life-giving for you and a "-" sign next to the roles that are most life-drain-

Framing a personal rule of life begins with identifying your primary roles and their corresponding relationships. Questions 1-3 are a great way to begin this process. Be honest and transparent. You will not be graded or judged by what you write down. The best way to approach all of the formative questions throughout this book is to jot down the first ideas that come to mind. You will have time later on to distill into finer prose any of the exercises you complete in this process.

This first set of questions is designed to help you frame your personal rule of life with a focus on roles and relationships. Remain attentive to any emotions that emerge as you write about the key persons in your life—those that evoke joy as well as sadness, remorse, concern or need. Don't assume that all roles and relationships are life-giving; some may in fact be the opposite, and that's perfectly acceptable—and very normal.

ing. Include helpful, descriptive commentary. Also place a star next to the roles that, for whatever reason, require special attention at this time. What is God inviting you to consider for each of your primary roles today?

4. From the list you have developed, identify your five (up to seven if you must!) most important roles (in order of priority) with key relationships named in each. If you have more than five (or seven) roles, prioritize the remaining roles and determine if any of these can be eliminated or minimized for the sake of discovering better life balance. Be as specific as possible about each role (e.g., father, husband and brother rather than "family man").

Take time now in questions 4-6 to begin working on this segment of your overarching personal rule of life statements. Don't expect to create a final draft the first time around. In this first section (when we cover the larger life defining topics of roles, gifts, desires, vision and mission), you will be asked specific questions to reveal each major area under consideration. As you progress in developing your personal rule of life, you'll return to these foundational statements frequently so their life-giving nature will not only be planted in your souls but germinate, grow, be pruned and blossom forth to God's glory.

5. Prayerfully consider how God might be inviting you to focus on your top roles and key relationships during this season of your life. Are there specific issues you need to attend to within your particular roles or relationships at this time?

6. Inquire of the Lord how best to tend to your own emotional health; write down any specific ideas you wish to consider in prioritizing your emotional needs. Be honest about this and reflect on your current emotional health and how that's affecting the quality of your relationships and your participation therein. If you feel led to say no to others in order to tend to your own needs, be sure to approach this humbly and willingly. If you discover in this reflection that you are sad, depressed, angry or anxious, consult the aid of a professional counselor, pastor or spiritual leader to attend to your current emotional needs.

Spiritual Community

1. In what way does the story of King David resonate with you? Why?

2. In what way does the faithfulness of C. S. Lewis toward his primary rules and relationships most encourage you? Why?

3. As you read about both David and Lewis, what in their stories sparked within you a desire to retool your roles and focus more on the key relationships in your life?

4. What is the overall state of your personal relationships? Talk about a key relationship needing extra attention during this season of life. What do you hope to focus on as a result of your individual reflections in this section?

5. How many roles have you identified for yourself? Do you believe this is the appropriate number to be carrying during this season of life? Which are most life-giving, and which require the most attention and why?

Thank you, Lord, for the ways you fashion my life around relationships. Were it not for my family and friends, I would find myself so alone in this world. As I continue to reflect on the quality of my relationships, help me identify ways I can continually be a positive contributor to the health and well-being of others. May the love, mercy, grace and compassion of Jesus be my daily source of strength and hope. I long to be your ambassador of peace and reconciliation in my family, among my friendships, and in the various communities where you lead me to love and serve others. In your name Father, Son and Holy Spirit, and for your kingdom's sake. Amen.

2

GIFTS

What Are My God-Given Gifts, Talents and Temperament?

Guiding Principle

Gifts: **Your personal rule of life is discerned and framed through the discovery of your spiritual gifts, natural talents and temperament.**

As you observe the people you most admire, how have you in the past week or month seen one of these individuals share their gifts or talents in service to others? If you're willing, share with him or her what you notice and affirm that person for willingly utilizing God's gift for the sake of another person (jot some of your observations here).

> *We are all missionaries. Wherever we go, we either bring people nearer to Christ, or we repel them from Christ. I believe that God made me for a purpose, but He also made me fast. When I run, I feel His pleasure.*
> —ERIC H. LIDDELL, *CHARIOTS OF FIRE*

As you consider your heroes who are no longer living, what is it about them that placed them in your "hero" category? What were their gifts and abilities, and how were these evidenced in their daily lives?

Note here what you believe to be your greatest contributions to the lives of those around you. What gifts and talents do you manifest most distinctively today, and how is your temperament a contributor to sharing those with others?

Biblical Reflection

For by the grace given me I say to every one of you: Do not think of yourself more highly than you ought, but rather think of yourself with sober judgment, in accordance with the measure of faith God has given you. Just as each of us has one body with many members, and these members do not all have the same function, so in Christ we who are many form one body, and each member belongs to all the others. We have different gifts, according to the grace given us. If a man's gift is prophesying, let him use it in proportion to his faith. If it is serving, let him serve; if it is teaching, let him teach; if it is encouraging, let him encourage; if it is contributing to the needs of others, let him give generously; if it is leadership, let him govern diligently; if it is showing mercy, let him do it cheerfully. (Romans 12:3-8)

In Romans 12, Ephesians 4 and 1 Corinthians 12, the apostle Paul describes for us, the people of God, how we are to be filled up with the Spirit and exercise the gifts imparted to us as his offspring. In each of these passages we discover how the lavish love of the Father is bestowed on his children. No one in the family of God is exempt or forgotten—all have been granted both natural and supernatural gifts and abilities, as well as temperaments and personalities suited to fulfill each one.

As Paul outlines in each of the major gifts passages (although not exhaustively or exclusively seen in each), the gifts are to be garnered from deep within the heart of the believer and then released through the faithful life of a servant. All are given for God's glory, the building up of the kingdom of God and the strengthening of the church. None are offered merely to enjoy or engage in isolation, but each are granted to us for the advancement of others and the encouragement of many. Some are used for expressing hard truths in

ways that exhort and challenge. Others are designed to edify and affirm.

From Romans 12:6-8 we discover the gifts of prophecy, ministry, service, teaching, exhortation, encouragement, giving, leading, showing mercy and compassion. In Ephesians 4:11 we see the fivefold ministry gifts of apostle, prophet, evangelist, pastor and teacher. First Corinthians 12:1-14 outlines nine spiritual gifts: wisdom, knowledge, faith, healing, miraculous powers, prophecy, discerning various spirits, speaking in tongues and interpretation of tongues.

In addition, 1 Corinthians 12:28-31 introduces apostle, prophet, teacher, workers of miracles, healing, helping others, administration and speaking in tongues. Other miscellaneous passages from the New Testament bring out celibacy (1 Corinthians 7), hospitality (1 Peter 4:9-10), martyrdom (1 Corinthians 13:1-3), missionary (Ephesians 3:6-8) and voluntary poverty (1 Corinthians 13:1-3). Still others can be found in the

Old Testament, which includes crafts-manship (Exodus 35:30-35; 1 Chronicles 22:15-16), worship (gift of musical expression and the leadership of others; Exodus 15), and the interpretation of dreams (Genesis 40–41).

> In truth, we cannot become anything other than who we already are, if we wish to be fulfilled in our lives and vocation. We must stop trying to "become" something else, or to "develop" or "cultivate" some trait that we fundamentally lack, and instead start being who we already are by identifying our giftedness and living it out.

Our gifts and talents all come from the hand of almighty God. We can't claim them as our own, as if we created or designed them by ancestry or practice. But each of us has a responsibility to know what they are and lean into them with an earnest desire to develop them throughout our lives. With the help of our spiritual friends and several good online tools that aid us in the process, discovering our gifts is a rather straightforward process.

Our temperaments are also innate rather than learned. Our introversion or extroversion, for example, are definitive qualities of our personhood created by God while we were in our mother's womb (Psalm 139). We acknowledge our true selves when we appreciate the way that God made us. This includes the specific gifts, talents and temperaments that are part of God's design in order to fulfill the purpose he has for our lives. In addition to the life-transforming nature of God's Word, there are many resources available to us that help unlock the truth about ourselves and set us free to become all we're meant to be.

The more we discover about God, the more we learn about ourselves and vice versa. Self-understanding and God awareness go hand in glove. We are not separated from the way God uniquely designed us; nor is our growing intimacy with God distinct from our ever-deepening self-discovery. Exploring both will lead us into the fullness of our life in the Spirit.

However, even though we may look at lists of spiritual gifts and take inventories to discover and affirm the gifts, talents and temperaments God has granted to us, the most important indicators of their validity come from within our hearts, from the affirmation of others and from the fruitfulness they produce in others. God is honored throughout the process of defining and refining them, and he is glorified as they are fully embraced and released in and through us and within the context of the body of Christ.

That's what Paul was doing when he encouraged Timothy, his son in the faith. Paul encouraged him to be bold in exercising his gifts, in embracing and unleashing the temperament given to him since birth, and all for the glory of God. These two men had a special bond of fellowship, Paul as the spiritual father in the Lord and Timothy his beloved child in the faith (1 Timothy 1:2, 18). Paul thanks God constantly for Timothy, remembering his tears with joy, longing day and night that Timothy may be filled with joy, and encouraging him to have a spirit of power, love and self-control (2 Timothy 1:2-7). To Paul, there was "no one else like him" (Philippians 2:19-22) who served with him in the spreading of the gospel. Timothy was both teachable and trustworthy to teach many others.

Timothy was first introduced to Paul in Acts 16:1-3, where we learn that his mother, Eunice, was Jewish and his father was Greek. Because he was so highly regarded in Lystra and Iconium, Paul wanted this young disciple to accompany him on his travels. Paul had him circumcised in order to accommodate the ministry they were having among the Jews. This began a long relationship of serving side by side. Not only did they travel together, but Paul trusted Timothy enough to leave him behind in various cities to proclaim the gospel of Jesus Christ as well as to establish new local fellowships (Acts 17:13-14). Timothy also assisted his spiritual father by going back to encourage the congregation in Thessalonica (1 Thessalonians 3:1-3), Philippi (Philippians 2:19-24) and Corinth (1 Corinthians 16:10-11).

Paul was Timothy's role model and example of faithfulness in fully releasing the gifts that God had bestowed on him. In 2 Timothy 3:10-15 Paul reminds Timothy:

You, however, know all about my teaching, my way of life, my purpose, faith, patience, love, endurance, persecutions, sufferings—what kinds of things happened to me in Antioch, Iconium and Lystra, the persecutions I endured. Yet the Lord rescued me from all of them. In fact, everyone who wants to live a godly life in Christ Jesus will be persecuted, while evil men and impostors will go from bad to worse, deceiving and being deceived. But as for you, continue in what you have learned and have become convinced of, because you know those from whom you learned it, and how from infancy you have known the holy Scriptures, which are able to make you wise for salvation through faith in Christ Jesus.

All of us have spiritual gifts and natural talents. When our talents are used for the glory of God and the building up of his church, they are enhanced by the ministry of God's Spirit. Do they turn into spiritual gifts as a result? Not really. Those special gifts that come from the loving hand of God are in this category. Talents are distinct from gifts. But when we use our talents for God's purposes and for his glory, the result is often the same as when we employ our spiritual gifts. The key is to learn how to give back to the Lord all that we are and are becoming—living sacrifices holy and acceptable to God and fragrant offerings to the world he invites us to serve in his name.

While there are differences between a natural talent and a spiritual gift, both can be used by God. When properly and obediently delivered—used for the glory of God and the good of others—they can be multiplied a hundredfold and produce life in others. The key here is not to split hairs about the difference between a talent and a gift but instead to give all that we have and are back to our Maker, Redeemer and Sustainer, fully released for the glory of God.

1. The apostle Paul, who authored most of the texts dealing with the spiritual gifts, obediently used the gifts entrusted to him by God throughout his ministry. It's interesting that 1 Corinthians 13, the love chapter, follows the longest list of spiritual gifts provided by Paul. Sit with 1 Corinthians 13 and ponder prayerfully how and why love is the "most excellent way" to be members of the body of Christ and to exercise the gifts of God's Spirit well. Jot down any ideas that pop off the page and into your heart, and consider afresh how your own temperament is unleashed as you exhibit love.

2. Imagine being Timothy, the one so deeply loved by the apostle Paul. Consider Paul's charge to Timothy in 2 Timothy 3:10–4:8. What do you notice about these invitations and exhortations? Which are particularly significant for you? Why?

3. Paul wrote to the church in Philippi,

> I hope in the Lord Jesus to send Timothy to you soon, that I also may be cheered when I receive news about you. I have no one else like him, who takes a genuine interest in your welfare. For everyone looks out for his own interests, not those of Jesus Christ. But you know that Timothy has proved himself, because as a son with his father he has served with me in the work of the gospel. I hope, therefore, to send him as soon as I see how things go with me. And I am confident in the Lord that I myself will come soon. (Philippians 2:19-24)

Why did Paul have to say that Timothy "proved himself" in his work for the gospel? How does the full expression of our spiritual gifts "prove" our faithfulness as servants of the gospel?

Historical Insight

When we utilize our gifts within the context of our calling as Christians, we either bring people nearer to Christ or we repel them from him. This certainly rings true for all, regardless of what our gifts, talents and temperament may be.

Phillis Wheatley was a woman with incredible gifts, and she freely offered them to others. Wheatley was the first published African American poet, and her writings helped to create the genre of African American literature. When she wrote poetry, she felt the Father's pleasure.

Phillis first came to America on July 11, 1761, one of a shipload of slaves sent to stand on the auction block in Boston, Massachusetts. She was a frail West African girl, only eight years old at that time. Brutally snatched from her homeland, she had no idea of the extraordinary life she would encounter in America. She was purchased by the Wheatley family and named after her slave ship, the *Phillis*. The Wheatleys were conscious of her tender age and sympathetic to her poor health, so they treated her with kindness. She was assigned to serve as the personal attendant to Mrs. Susanna Wheatley and given the task of basic household duties.

In the Wheatley household she grew up both as a slave and as a young woman. Mary Wheatley, the daughter of the family, enjoyed Phillis's company and taught her English, Latin and religion. She also introduced her to good literature.

Apparently quite brilliant and with an aptitude for learning, Phillis soon acquired an education that any free young woman from a well-off family of that time would envy. She became an avid student of the Bible and especially admired the works of Alexander Pope (1688-1744), the British neoclassical writer. Through Pope's translation of Homer, she also developed a taste for Greek mythology. Thus was launched a remarkable career as a poet and a life of deep religious piety for young Phillis.

On December 21, 1767, the fourteen-year-old Wheatley had her first poem published in the *Newport* (Rhode Island) *Mercury*. This amazing achievement came only six years after her arrival in America, without any prior knowledge of the English language. However, it was really her poem "On the Death of Rev. Mr. George Whitefield" that launched Wheatley into public prominence. Whitefield was a well-known minister and evangelist in America and Britain at that time. Since the Wheatleys were especially fond of Whitefield's preaching ministry, this must have been meaningful for them. This elegy became Phillis's poetic trademark. Twenty of the forty-six poems published in her lifetime were about death—a subject she embraced as a Christian because of its central importance to understanding our eternal hope. Here is an excerpt from her Whitefield poem:

HAIL, happy saint, on thine
    immortal throne,
Possest of glory, life, and bliss
    unknown;
We hear no more the music of thy
    tongue,
Thy wonted auditories cease to
    throng.
Thy sermons in unequall'd accents
    flow'd,
And ev'ry bosom with devotion
    glow'd;
Thou didst in strains of eloquence
    refin'd
Inflame the heart, and captivate the
    mind.

There is no doubt Wheatley's poetry commands a respectable place among the eighteenth-century American poets. However, since it was so hard for Americans of the time to believe that an African woman could write such excellent poetry, in 1772 Phillis had to defend her literary ability in court. She was examined by a group of Boston luminaries, including John Erving; Rev. Charles Chauncey; John Hancock; Thomas Hutchinson, the governor of Massachusetts; and his lieutenant governor Andrew Oliver. They concluded that indeed she was the author of the poetry ascribed to her name "and signed an attestation which was published in the preface to her book Poems on Various Subjects, Religious and Moral published in Aldgate, London, in 1773. The book was published in London because publishers in Boston had refused to publish the text."

In addition to elegies, Wheatley wrote on religious, classical and abstract themes. She rarely mentions her own situation in her poems, most likely because she was so young when she was stolen out of Africa and because of her humility as a young woman of God. One of the few poems she writes that refers to her experience as a slave is from "On being brought from Africa to America." In this poem she writes:

Twas mercy brought me from my
    Pagan land,
Taught my benighted soul to
    understand
That there's a God, that there's a
    Saviour too:
Once I redemption neither sought
    nor knew.
Some view our sable race with
    scornful eye,
"Their colour is a diabolic dye."

In every circumstance, Phillis Wheatley gave all the glory to God and claimed none of her success for herself. It's obvious that the strong Christian influence of the Wheatley family and her roots as a humble young woman led to her deep Christian piety. Her spiritual formation earned her the respect and endearment of all the distinguished people she encountered, including George Washington, with whom she had an audience when she sent him a letter and poem on the impending war, as well as several leaders in England. Her gifts as a poet were used for the glory of God. Her temperament and her self-effacing ways were endearing to all who knew and loved her.

By October 1773 Phillis was a free woman, emancipated by the Wheatley family one month after Susanna Wheatley's death. On April 1, 1778, she married John Peters, a free black man. They had three children, though none survived. Her young adult years were filled with struggle. No longer supported financially by the Wheatley family, she was now in a financially strapped marriage herself, dealing with the death of each child she brought to life, and persevering through her own increasingly failing health. Through it all, however, Phillis Wheatley was never known to be discouraged.

Wheatley remained loyal to her benefactors and showed empathic concern for those in situations less fortunate that her own. She was especially sympathetic to the plight of slaves, condemning slavery indirectly in her poems. She loved her freedom despite the hardships that accompanied the challenge of living in America as a black woman. Phillis's Christian faith was the real key to freedom. The Bible was her favorite book, and her love for Jesus was the truth that set her free. Her belief that Christ would ultimately triumph over the world's problems led her to hope in eternal freedom forever. She died at the age of thirty-one on December 5, 1784.

A Hymn to the Evening
Soon as the sun forsook the eastern
    main
The pealing thunder shook the
    heav'nly plain;
Majestic grandeur! From the
    zephyr's wing,
Exhales the incense of the
    blooming spring,
Soft purl the streams, the birds
    renew their notes,
And through the air their mingled
    music floats.
Through all the heav'ns what
    beauteous dyes are spread!
But the west glories in the deepest red;
So may our breasts with every
    virtue glow,
The living temples of our God Below!
Fill'd with the praise of him who
    gives the light,
And draws the sable curtains of the
    night,
Let placid slumbers soothe each
    weary mind,
At morn to wake more heav'nly,
    more refin'd;
So shall the labors of the day begin
More pure, more guarded from the
    snares of sin.
Night's leaden scepter seals my
    drowsy eyes,
Then cease, my song, till fair
    Aurora rise.
—Phillis Wheatley

Personal Rule of Life

1. What are the top three to five activities in your life that are most life-giving for you? In contrast, what activities are most life-draining? In what ways does this reflect your self-awareness of the temperament God has created deep within you?

2. What do you consider to be your primary spiritual gifts? Reflect on the biblical passages already noted. Consider taking a spiritual gifts inventory. Ask a few friends who know you best and love you most to identify those areas of giftedness they appreciate about you. Do they match your self-understanding?

As you answer questions 1-3, consider afresh your own personal talents and spiritual gifts. Without overspiritualizing any of them, reflect on the life God has invited you to fulfill in the context of the specific gifts he has placed in your care. Remember that all our spiritual gifts (e.g., of mercy, teaching, administration, evangelist) and natural talents (e.g., cooking meals or building houses) are to be recognized and maximized for the glory of our almighty God and the benefit of his kingdom on earth.

3. What are the primary natural talents God has given to you to steward well in this life (e.g., cooking, athleticism, woodwork, crafts, singing, photography)? Which talents do you feel led to reinforce through further training, developing greater expertise or helping others utilize for themselves?

4. As you review your list of activities, gifts and talents, in what ways does your temperament factor into how you utilize or underutilize each of these? (E.g., if you are an introvert, how does each of your activities bring out your best or make you anxious or tired? Or as a "J" on the Myers-Briggs Type Indicator, how does the use of your spiritual gifts build or frustrate your need for closure? Or as a strong personality, how do you feel you are perceived in most of your service environments?) Do you need to better understand

Take time now to begin writing the personal rule of life statement regarding your gifts and talents.

the composite temperament that God has given to you? If so, what means can you use to gain understanding (e.g., through the Myers-Briggs, DISC, Enneagram or another available online tool designed to aid us in increasing our self-awareness)?

5. In what ways is God inviting you to use your primary spiritual gifts for serving others and glorifying the Father?

6. Write one to three sentences on how you wish to pursue deepening your self-understanding as it relates to your gifts, talents and temperament. What help or resources will you need in this process?

Spiritual Community

1. Timothy was privileged to have the apostle Paul fanning the flame of his spiritual gifts and celebrating how God was using him to build up the church. In what ways do these biblical reflections encourage you to "fan the flame" in others, possibly even within your group of spiritual friends?

2. As you read Phillis Wheatley's amazing story of redemption and emancipation, what aspect of her poetry tapped into your creativity and the use of your talents and gifts?

3. Reflecting on your personal insights regarding your gifts, talents and temperament, how will a growing self-awareness free you up to serve others?

4. What did you identify as your primary spiritual gifts, and how do you see them being used in the body of Christ today? In your exploration of the gifts in the biblical text, are you able to celebrate the gifts that God has specifically given to you?

5. How can we encourage one another to hone our natural talents, particularly those we enjoy the most?

6. In the coming week, how will you lean into the joy of developing these talents for your own enjoyment and the benefit of others?

Loving Father, you have richly blessed all of your children with both natural and Spirit-empowered gifts. As I have explored this topic for myself and within the context of my spiritual friends, help me to not only appreciate what I have observed in those around me, but begin afresh to see how you have lavished your love upon me. I long to both acknowledge and affirm that all good gifts come from your gracious hand. Guide me in this endeavor to magnify your holy name as I recognize and utilize the gifts you have generously given to me. I love you, Father. Amen.

DESIRES

What Are My Deepest Longings and Core Values?

❖

Guiding Principle

Desires: **Your personal rule of life is discerned and framed through the longings, yearnings and goals God has placed on your heart and mind that propel you forward with joy.**

As you read or hear about the news of the day, what recent current affairs (in politics, education, the economy, even sports or entertainment) bring a tear of empathy or joy to your eye, and what frightens, appalls or concerns you about one such real-life situation?

> *You have made us for yourself, and our heart is restless, until it rests in you.*
> —AUGUSTINE
>
> *The fundamental commandment, first in importance as well as in order, and basic to every other, is "You shall have no other gods before me." True religion starts with accepting this as one's rule of life.*
> —J. I. PACKER

As you think back to your childhood, what experiences did you have that taught you—for good or ill—how to respond to the needs of others, especially those who are wildly successful or desperately downtrodden? How have these experiences affected the way your longings and values have been shaped today?

Over the past few months, in what ways has God heard the cry of your heart toward an issue or personal concern? How did that pour courage into your heart and build up your faith? Or in what ways are you experiencing dryness or darkness, and you haven't sensed God hearing the deep cries of your heart? How has that affected your life of faith today? It's okay to be honest; God can handle it!

Biblical Reflection

Trust in the LORD and do good;
  dwell in the land and enjoy safe pasture.
Delight yourself in the LORD
  and he will give you the desires of your heart.
(Psalm 37:3-4)

What does the psalmist mean when he writes that God will give you the desires of your heart? According to John Piper,

> The opposite of wasting your life is living life by a single God-exalting, soul-satisfying passion. The well-lived life must be God-exalting and soul-satisfying because that is why God created us (Isaiah 43:7; Psalm 90:14). And "passion" is the right word (or, if you prefer, zeal, fervor, ardor, blood-earnestness) because God commands us to love him with all our heart (Matthew 22:37), and Jesus reminds us that he spits luke-warm people out of his mouth (Revelation 3:16). The opposite of wasting your life is to live by a single, soul-satisfying passion for the supremacy of God in all things.

Once our lives are touched by the gospel, there's no turning back. Otherwise, the life of the Spirit is replaced once more by the life of the flesh, a life of idolatry (preferring other gods to the one true God). It's the ongoing plight of the beloved to continually wrestle with the flesh in order for the Spirit to reign supreme over the fleshly desires that lurk so close to the surface of our hearts. We all face this in common and will continue to do so for the rest of our earthly lives.

Our core values are shaped by our pasts and informed by our biblical convictions; subsequently they feed our longings and desires for more of God. He must increase and we must decrease (as John the Baptist once declared). Our desires are to align with God's desires; they should complement and not compete with the life-transforming gospel we claim to embody in this life.

The apostle Peter embodied the gospel. We can gain much about godly desires and biblical values from his example.

The Bible doesn't tell us much about Peter's life before he encountered Jesus.

We don't know too much about his family life or his fishing abilities. But we do know that after encountering the Lord, Jesus called him "the Rock" (Peter), and his passions were enlarged. No longer a fisherman, he was now a fisher of humans. Gone were the days of hauling fish for profit. Now he focused on catching men and women, young and old, for the kingdom of God. His encounter with Christ transformed his passions and values—he was sold out for Jesus.

Peter was a man of passion, which, when combined with the gifts and temperament God had given him since childhood, made him a spiritual force to reckon with. Known for his incredible verbal gaffs and dramatic missteps around Jesus, he was also the obvious leader of the pack known as the Twelve. His weaknesses and strengths make him all the more accessible to the average Christian. We can all relate to the two sides of Peter—impulsive denier and devoted discipler wrapped up in one.

Simon Peter is referred to nearly two hundred times in the New Testament (the beloved disciple John is mentioned about thirty times). He was a Galilean fisherman by trade (John 1:40-42; Luke 5:10) and not formally educated (Acts 4:13). He was originally from Bethsaida but relocated to Capernaum. His brother Andrew introduced him to Jesus (John 1:35-42). He was married (Matthew 8:14) and had a large home (two stories, enough to house his family and his mother-in-law). We don't know the name of Peter's wife, but we do know she joined him on some of his missionary trips (1 Corinthians 9:5).

Peter was a leader among the disciples (Matthew 10:2). His name is always listed first among the disciples. Peter was in the core group of three disciples, including James and John (Mark 5:37; 9:2; 14:33). He was the first to perceive Jesus as Messiah (Matthew 16:17-19), first to be called by name by Jesus (John 1:40-42), first to confess his sinfulness to Jesus (Luke 5:8), and first to promise never to desert Jesus (Mark 14:27-31). When a question arises about the temple tax, the collectors come to Peter (Matthew 17:24). In addition, he receives the most serious rebukes from Jesus, and at least seven miracles of Jesus were performed for Peter or connected to him (two miraculous catches of fish, the curing of his mother-in-law, his walking on water, the healing of Malchus's ear, the two miraculous deliverances from prison, and the coin in the fish's mouth). Besides Jesus, Peter is the most prominent and central figure of the Gospels.

His passionate friendship with Jesus is obvious throughout the Gospels. Like most friendships, there are mishaps and misspoken words that form a deep bond between these two men. Jesus made a radical difference in Peter's life, and his allegiance to and alliance with the Savior comes in all shapes, sizes and forms. At the transfiguration he asks to erect shelters (Mark 9:5), one for Jesus and the other two for Elijah and Moses, an idea that came more from fear than wisdom. He's the only disciple to attempt to walk on water, albeit unsuccessfully (Matthew 14:28-31). He was the first to deny Jesus

(Luke 22:21-23; 31-34; 54-71) as well as the first to be restored to Jesus (John 21:15-19). It is important to point out that Jesus reinstated Peter by asking him three questions. These questions gave Peter the opportunity to proclaim his love for Jesus three times, which is the same number of times he denied Christ.

In essence, the story of the foot washing (John 13:1-17) focuses on the interaction between Jesus and Peter. The others are present, but the apex of the scene focuses on Peter's intimate encounter with Jesus. Peter inquires, "Lord, are you going to wash my feet?" and then responds, "No, you shall never wash my feet." But Jesus immediately corrects him, "Unless I wash you, you have no part of me," to which Peter retorts, "Then not just my feet but my hands and my head as well!" Here is the perfect example of Peter's impetuous nature getting in the middle of an important encounter with the Savior. As a result, the intensity of their love for one another strengthens.

After Christ was crucified and resurrected, Peter was the first to enter the empty tomb (running there with the beloved disciple John [John 20:6-7]). As a result of believing with certainty the truth about the resurrected Jesus, he became the primary leader of the early church. He proposed replacing Judas in Acts 1:15-26; preached the first Pentecost sermon in Acts 2:14-36; performed the first healing in Acts 3:6; defended the gospel before the Sanhedrin in Acts 4:8-12; decided the case of Ananias and Sapphira in Acts 5:1-11; and mediated between James and Paul in Acts 15:5-11. He received a magnificent vision of the unity of God's people (Acts 10–11). After his miraculous release from prison (Acts 12:1-17), Peter left Jerusalem and devoted himself to missionary work (Acts 12:18-19; 15; Galatians 2:7-8; 1 Corinthians 1:12; 9:5; 1–2 Peter).

The biblical evidence is sufficient for us to acknowledge that Peter was both a man of deep passion and spiritual power. His life, ministry, gifts, temperament and calling place him in the center of the Gospels. His heart for Jesus and the transformation he experienced is dramatically significant for the first-century church and for all Christ followers today. May his desires, longings and passions for the body of Christ be released within each of us who desire to be used of God for his greater glory.

1. Peter was the first among equals in the band of brothers who accompanied Jesus all the way to the cross. He was a passionate friend and companion of Jesus, and a leader of the early church. When Jesus invited him and his companions to follow him, "they pulled their boats up on shore, left everything and followed him" (Luke 5:11). Reflect on the significance of this immediate response to Jesus' invitation.

2. Peter's life represents discipleship for all who belong to the Christian community.

   Peter's pastoral commission flows out of his own fragile discipleship. He must repent, return to his love for the Lord, and then strengthen and feed others (Luke 22:32; John 21:15-17). The New Testament authors also remind us that discipleship will mean his suffering like Jesus did. Both Peter's resistance to the message of the cross (Mark 8:31-33) and his boast that he would lay down his life for Jesus (John 13:37) describe partial truths about Peter's life. Peter is both "rock" (Matthew 16:18) and "stumbling block" (Matthew 16:23). Thus, Peter as disciple in the New Testament exhibits the ambiguities that many Christians feel in today's church.

   What is the significance of Peter being a stumbling block which prepared him to become the rock?

3. Peter was the first to deny Jesus as well as the first to be restored to him. Read John 21:15-19 and reflect on the three questions Jesus asks Peter. In what ways do these reinstate Peter into the inner circle, and what do you think is the significance of Jesus hearing Peter's renewed proclamation of love? What do these questions evoke in your own soul?

Historical Insight

A historical figure of great influence in twentieth-century Christianity was the passionately focused Harold John Ockenga. He was born June 6, 1905, in Chicago to Herman and Angie Ockenga. His mother was a devout Christian and raised her children accordingly by instilling in them a love for God, the Scriptures and the beauty of creation. The priorities of her life, as related to Harold, were "'to attend strictly to duty,' to 'take all disappointments graciously,' to attend worship and prayer meetings regularly, and to 'try and live [a] more holy [life].'"

At the age of eleven, during the summer of 1916, Ockenga was converted during an old-fashioned Methodist camp meeting in Illinois. Harold was convinced that this was the moment his sins were forgiven, but his life was yet to be completely transformed. It wasn't until some of Harold's friends invited him to a New Year's Eve (1922) Christian conference, sponsored by Knox College, that Ockenga heard a message that transformed his life. After the message Ockenga, with his friends, knelt down to pray together, and this is when "I covenanted with God that if he would save me I would preach the gospel." It was on this evening that he committed himself to becoming a passionate preacher instead of a trial lawyer, which he had anticipated all his life.

Ockenga attended Taylor University, and there he developed his gift of preaching and was challenged and sharpened in the areas of relationships. He was a leader of the Taylor University Evangelistic Team and would often spend entire nights in prayer with other team members. He was also a member of the Holiness League, a campus group that met every Friday evening for "prayer, fellowship, and mutual edification." In September 1927 Ockenga began graduate theological studies at Princeton Theological Seminary. However, two years into his program, in the summer of 1929, the Princeton faculty split and many left to establish Westminster Theological Seminary. Ockenga left Princeton to attend Westminster, and by doing so he left "an assured degree, an assured Fellowship which would send me to Europe, and all the material advantages." After graduating from Westminster in 1930, Ockenga took a job as a pastor in Pittsburgh and also completed his doctorate at the University of Pittsburgh. In 1934, while studying for his comprehensive exams in the Pitt library, Harold met Audrey Williamson, and on August 6, 1935, he and Audrey were married.

Ockenga eventually left his pastorate

in Pittsburgh, and on November 18, 1936, was installed as copastor of Park Street Church in Boston, Massachusetts. While at Park Street, Ockenga soared to national prominence as a leader of evangelical Christians. He devoted himself to worldwide evangelization, missions and resisting the influence of modernism. He also networked and developed relationships with leaders in the Evangelistic Association of New England (known today as Vision New England) and the New England Fellowship, and was elected as the first president of the National Association of Evangelicals.

During the middle of the twentieth century there was a growing movement of youth ministries, including such organizations as the Navigators (1933), Young Life Campaign (1941), Youth for Christ (1944), Fellowship of Christian Athletes (1954) and Youth With A Mission (1960). Youth for Christ fostered a wide network of deep friendships in which the likes of Ockenga, Billy Graham and Merv Rosell worked together. As a result of being "often thrown together at youth rallies, revival meetings, or summer conferences, they came to know and trust each other." The result: "by the mid-1940s a recognizable 'band of brothers' was beginning to emerge within the evangelical movement. While they all had their own personalities and styles, to be sure, they were drawn together by intense loyalties, deep friendships, and a shared mission." They shared a common longing—the proclamation of the gospel.

Through this band of brothers the Lord

cultivated many ministries that led to the revival and renewal of the church. For instance, Ockenga invited Graham to speak at a massive revival of over six thousand people in Mechanics Hall, Boston, on December 31, 1949. Graham also spoke a number of other times in the following weeks, culminating with a sixteen-thousand-person crowd at the Boston Garden. Later in April 1950, Graham preached to approximately fifty thousand people on the Boston Common. During the crusades of 1950 Graham spoke to over 1.5 million people and nearly fifty thousand were converted. Ockenga's passionate leadership was behind all of this success.

Ockenga and his fellow leaders of the mid-twentieth-century revivals shared core values: *reclaim the culture* through the reformation of society, including confronting racial prejudice, poverty, war and alcohol abuse; and *renew the mind*, through the establishment of institutions such as the Boston School of the Bible, Conferences for the Advancement of Evangelical Scholarship, Fuller Theological Seminary, *Christianity Today* and Gordon-Conwell Theological Seminary.

In addition to reclaiming culture and renewing the mind Ockenga's deepest desire, his deepest longing, yearning and goal was to *reach the world* via "heaven sent revival." Ockenga's preaching and teaching were often illustrated with reference to great revivals throughout history. In one lecture, given at Dallas Theological Seminary Ockenga said,

We are experiencing the mercy drops of God's blessings but we await the great revival. . . . What is the great revival? . . . It is the time when God's work is unusually prospered, quickened, enlarged, and vitalized. The normal, usual, expected progress of Christian work may be witnessed in many places. The great revival is only witnessed periodically in Christian history. The great revival marks a condition when men give primary interest and attention to the things of God above their livelihood, above their intellectual pursuits, and above their social interests. A terror of wrongdoing descends upon them. A passion for repentance seizes them. A desire for salvation characterizes them.

Ockenga was absorbed in revival literature and history, evidenced by the fact that books about Christianity's great revivals and their leaders filled the bookshelves in his library. In fact Ockenga even said, "All progress in Christian things is made by revivals." Ockenga was fascinated by the tremendous influence revivals have over both the church and the broader culture. He knew America needed revival, and he constantly prayed and worked toward it.

The revival Ockenga earnestly prayed for is called the "New England Mid-Century Revival," which began in Boston with Graham and Ockenga. It later spread across America and around the globe. In the midst of the revival Ockenga passionately sought to "reclaim the culture," "renew the mind" and "reach the world" with the gospel. The desires of his heart were realized first as seedlings of renewal in his lifetime and subsequently over the decades in the expansive growth experienced in the church. It's remarkable to consider the fruit of a life focused on the yearnings and goals placed in the heart by God.

Personal Rule of Life

1. What are the deepest desires and longings of your heart today? Without reservation, list all that come to your heart and mind—the sky's the limit! For the sake of making a faith-filled and honorable commitment to Christ, pay attention to those excellent, God-honoring desires that are to be fed, not to inappropriate, God-dishonoring desires (self-centered wants) that need to be starved.

   When answering questions 1-3, be honest and transparent as you identify the significant longings and desires of your heart that you trust have been placed there by God. Pay attention to the passions and yearnings that inform your daily convictions and have led you into areas of relationship and service with others. Acknowledge the longings of your heart with a deep sense of God's strong hand of blessing and assurance.

2. What matters most to you today? As a child of God, what are the core values that serve as the foundation for your relationships, responsibilities and decision making? Without discrimination, list all that matter most to you—don't hold back.

3. Are your desires and core values in congruence with the way you are currently living? In other words, if a core value is honesty or transparency, is this evidenced in your primary relationships, or are you holding back for some reason? What would need to change in order for you to fully attend to your core values and the deepest desires of your heart?

4. Go back to your list of desires (see 1) and prioritize them. Then list the top three to five here. Reflect on this list and note anything that might be missing—add or edit accordingly.

In questions 4-6, begin writing the following personal rule of life statement as it is related to your desires, passions and goals. Don't expect to create a final draft the first time around. As you progress in developing your personal rule of life, remember that we will often return to these foundational statements so that their life-giving nature can be planted in your soul to germinate, grow, be pruned and blossom forth for God's glory.

5. Go back to your list of core values (see 2) and prioritize them. Then, list the top three to five here. How does this list look to you? Anything missing or need to be edited?

6. In SMART goal language (a SMART goal is Specific, pointed and direct; Measurable, can be measured; Achievable, within reach and possible; Results orientated, answers why; Timed, with a clear start and end time), write out at least one key goal related to how you sense God is inviting you to make a change in your life today that would reflect more significantly one or more of your top desires.

Spiritual Community

1. Consider together Peter's threefold denial and his subsequent threefold proclamation of love. In what ways do you see such flip-flopping of the heart within the wider Christian community and within yourself?

2. Harold John Ockenga and his contemporaries had a passion to reclaim the culture,

renew the mind and reach the world. Which of these three areas are you most drawn to, and why?

3. As you consider the life of Peter, the passionate disciple of Jesus, and Ockenga, a passionate man of God in the twentieth century, how do their stories inspire you to become more passionate for witnessing to the kingdom of God?

4. What was it like for you to identify the deepest longings and desires of your heart? Was it the first time you've done so, or did it feel strange to be given permission to go to that place in your heart once again?

5. What are two to three core values that you identified in this exercise? In what ways do they reflect your spiritual or personal convictions? Do you think they apply to others, and if so, how will you communicate these to those you share life with most intimately today?

Lord, I often find it difficult to sort out my desires and longings. Which are of my own selfish wants and perceived needs, and which are clearly of you? I read the psalmist's words that you delight to grant me the desires and longings of my heart, but I find that my heart is often divided, restless and insecure. As I have sorted through the material in this chapter, I invite you, Father, Son and Holy Spirit, to have your way in my heart. Help me to identify the passions that you have clearly placed there, that solidify my understanding of your infallible Word and that reflect your purposeful passion for all which you have lovingly created. Make my longings fit for your praise, glory and delight. For the honor of your Name, the building up of your kingdom and all for Christ's sake. Amen.

VISION

What Is the Intentional Passion
God Has Planted in Me?

❖

Guiding Principle

Vision: **Your personal rule of life is discerned and framed within the holistic, long-term vision and passion God has planted in your heart.**

If you were asked by a dear friend to state in one sentence (or several words or phrases) what you believe are your unique big-picture contributions to the world around you, what would you say?

The place God calls you to is the place where your deep gladness and the world's deep hunger meet.
—FREDERICK BUECHNER,
LISTENING TO YOUR LIFE

If that same friend were to inquire about what makes you most passionate about your daily life and service to others, what words or phrases would you use?

Much bigger than a career, job or occupation, our unique calling will be based on our gifts and abilities, will grow out of our deepest desires, and will always involve some response to the needs of the world.
—GORDON T. SMITH,
COURAGE AND CALLING

As you embark on the journey toward a deeper sense of calling and commitment to fulfill God's distinct vision by releasing passion from deep within you, what is the prayer of your heart?

Biblical Reflection

**The LORD came and stood there, calling as at other times, "Samuel! Samuel!"
Then Samuel said, "Speak, for your servant is listening." (1 Samuel 3:10)**

Your unique vocational calling is like a thumbprint or snowflake: we all have similar characteristics but an individual design and purpose. The biblical story offers several illustrations of those who discovered their unique calling (some over time and others more spontaneously and miraculously) and others who unfortunately missed it along the way.

The vision of God comes to his people in various ways. In this section we will examine several biblical characters but will concentrate on the life of Moses. Look for ways that Moses' story compares to yours, and remain open to how God is inviting you into a more intimate vision and passionate vocational call.

But first a few other examples.

Adam and Eve were in the Garden, and the Lord spoke his vision clearly to Adam saying, "You are free to eat from any tree in the garden; but you must not eat from the tree of knowledge of good and evil, for when you eat of it you will surely die" (Genesis 2:16-17). How hard would it have been to obey such a direct and specific command from God?

Noah was a righteous man, blameless among the people of his time. Noah walked with God (Genesis 6:9) and fulfilled his unique calling, which was to build an ark to protect his family from the floodwaters of God's judgment on the earth. "Noah did everything just as God commanded him" (Genesis 6:22). He was asked to use his roles, passion and talents to fulfill a unique call—to build an ark. Noah heard the vision and obeyed to completion.

Abram heard God's call:

Leave your country, your people and your father's household and go to the land I will show you.

I will make you into a great nation
  and I will bless you;
I will make your name great,
  and you will be a blessing.
  (Genesis 12:1-2)

So, Abram left, as the Lord told him to, and a great nation was established.

Joseph was one of Abraham's great-great grandsons. Jacob's son Joseph had a dream (Genesis 37) that would frustrate his brothers and ultimately catapult him into reigning over Egypt and serving alongside Pharaoh as a wise and discerning leader (Genesis 38–50). Though Joseph was scorned and neglected by his brothers, he followed fervently after the visionary call of God.

Many generations later God called Samuel out for his service. When Samuel was conflicted by the sound of God's voice, thinking it was his mentor Eli (1 Samuel 3:8-9), he discovered something from God that would "make the ears of everyone who hears of it tingle" (1 Samuel 3:11). It was a hard message for Eli, but even he was willing to have the Lord "do what is good in his eyes" (1 Samuel 3:18). Hearing God's call comes out of an ability to hear his voice. Samuel, confused by what he at first thought was his elder's voice, listened well and obeyed. His response was, "Speak LORD, your servant is listening."

There are many other examples in the Bible that demonstrate for us how calling comes out of listening—hearing and responding to the voice of God. People like Gideon (Judges 6:14), who was called by God to save Israel out of Midian's hand; Elijah (1 Kings 19:12), who heard from God in a gentle whisper and who called Elisha (1 Kings 19:19) to follow him and serve as his attendant; Isaiah, who responded positively to God's question, "Whom shall I send? And who will go for me?" saying, "Here am I. Send me" (Isaiah 6:8). Then there's Ruth, Rahab, Esther, Daniel, Jonah, Saul, David, Solomon, Jeremiah and a host of others too numerous to mention at this time.

In the New Testament we have examples that begin with Elizabeth, who being empowered by the Spirit was called to birth John. Mary miraculously heard the call and was found to be with child by the Holy Spirit and eventually gave birth to our Lord Jesus. Peter was called away from his fishing nets to become the chief fisher of people. Paul was arrested by the Spirit, was called and set apart to proclaim the Word of life to the pagan world of his time. The examples are plentiful, and the truth is clear: God's clarion call is to all who claim his name, and the choice is before us: to listen and embrace or ig-

nore and miss it completely.

As you reflect on these illustrations of a handful of biblical characters, pause for a moment and consider your own life. In what ways has God been seeking to get your attention lately? Have there been people, circumstances or experiences that, upon reflection, are God's attempts to capture the attention of your heart? Think back over your past week, month, season or year; are there examples of God's initiative toward you that may in fact be contributors to his desires for you?

Speak, Lord, your servant is listening (jot down any reflections that come to your heart or mind).

We now fix our attention on the life of Moses. Moses at first resisted the call of God. His call came in the presence of a burning bush (Exodus 3:1-9). There the angel of the Lord appeared to him in flames of fire. How could Moses miss it? Calling him by name, God invited Moses to take off his sandals and stand barefoot on holy ground. Moses hid his face because he was so afraid to look at God. His call from God was specific: free the Hebrews from their misery in Egypt and take them up out of that land into a "good and spacious land, a land flowing with milk and honey" (Exodus 3:8).

He initially had all sorts of excuses for not fulfilling God's unique call on his life. In Exodus 3:11 he reminds God of his personal shortcomings: "Who am I, that I should go to Pharaoh and bring the Israelites out of Egypt?" In Exodus 4:1 he expresses his fears about the unbelief of the people: "What if they do not believe me or listen to me and say, 'The LORD did not appear to you'?" In Exodus 4:10 he stutters forth his lack of eloquence: "O Lord, I have never been eloquent, neither in the past nor since you have spoken to your servant. I am slow of speech and tongue." And, finally, in Exodus 4:13 he requests someone else to do the leading saying, "O Lord, please send someone else to do it."

Eventually Moses rose to the challenge of living for God and fulfilled his call with spiritual power and resolve. God promised and delivered aid to Moses through his divine presence and authority. All along the journey, even in the midst of plagues (water changing to blood, frogs, gnats, flies, livestock, boils, hail, locusts, darkness, etc.), Moses experienced intimacy with the Lord. We are told that "the LORD would speak to Moses face to face, as a man speaks with his friend" (Exodus 33:11). Out of this ever-deepening intimacy Moses' vision was continuously clarified and his passionate call was fulfilled.

He delivered the people miraculously out of Egypt, all by the strong guiding hand of almighty God. His role at Mount Sinai reveals the ongoing conversation between God and his chosen servant Moses (cf. Exodus 19, 20, 23, 24, 32–34). He was a beloved child of the King and holds a special place in the history of God's chosen ones. We are forever indebted to Moses for his willingness to be used of God in so many powerful ways. We learn from Moses' example that when God calls his people he gives them every resource necessary for understanding and implementing that call, even during hairpin turns of

confusion, seasons of desolation and the reality of disappointing relationships.

Moses' role in the biblical narrative is bigger than life. His contributions to the faith community are as important as they've ever been. One of the most notable is the receiving of the Ten Commandments:

> You shall have no other gods
>   before me.
> You shall not make for yourself
>   an idol . . .
> You shall not misuse the name of
>   the LORD your God . . .
> Remember the Sabbath day by
>   keeping it holy. . . .
> Honor your father and your
>   mother . . .
> You shall not murder.
> You shall not commit adultery.
> You shall not steal.
> You shall not give false testimony
>   against your neighbor.
> You shall not covet your neighbor's
>   house. (Exodus 20:3-17)

What is it about Moses' life and the fulfillment of his calling that encourages you to pursue your unique call, vision and passion for life and service? You may want to review Deuteronomy 32–33 for ideas about how best to envision the end of your life and the fulfillment of your call. The Song of Moses, found in Deuteronomy 32, is a powerful reflection on a life well lived in visionary service to God. Use the following for prayerful reflection:

> Let my teaching fall like rain
>   and my words descend like dew,
> like showers on new grass,

like abundant rain on tender
  plants. (v. 2)

He is the Rock, his works are perfect,
  and all his ways are just.
A faithful God who does no wrong,
  upright and just is he. (v. 4)

He shielded him and cared for him;
  he guarded him as the apple of
    his eye,
like an eagle that stirs up its nest
  and hovers over its young,
that spreads its wings to catch them
  and carries them aloft.
The LORD alone led him;
  no foreign god was with him.
    (vv. 10-12)

When Moses finished reciting all these words to all Israel, he said to them, "Take to heart all the words I have solemnly declared to you this day, so that you may command your children to obey carefully all the words of this law. They are not just idle words for you—they are your life. By them you will live long in the land you are crossing the Jordan to possess." (vv. 45-47)

What a gracious word to wrap up a life! Moses then handed the baton to Joshua, and his legacy of faithfulness continued to reap fruit for God's glory. The Bible reads, "Now Joshua son of Nun was filled with the spirit of wisdom because Moses had laid his hands on him. So the Israelites listened to him and did what the LORD had commanded Moses" (Deuteronomy 34:9).

1. Take a moment to consider the end of your own life. What would you like others to say of you as they express their final farewell? Why not begin that legacy today?

2. By what means did God make his call to Moses clear (Exodus 3:1-9)? Aaron is directed by God (Exodus 4:27) to meet Moses and come alongside him in his journey of faith. What was the collective response to God's call (Exodus 4:31)?

3. Review God's promises for deliverance (Exodus 6:1-8). What does God pledge to his people no matter what obstacles they may encounter (whatever may "plague" them!) (see Exodus 7–11)? After crossing the Red Sea, what was Moses' response (Exodus 15:1-18)?

4. On Mount Sinai (Exodus 19–20), Moses receives the Ten Commandments. In response, Moses says to the Lord, "Speak to us yourself and we will listen" (Exodus 20:19). What does the Lord say to them in response (Exodus 20:22-26)? On a second visit to Mount Sinai, Moses remained there for forty days (Exodus 24:18). Aaron and the people get impatient and build the golden calf (Exodus 32:1-6). In what ways is divine wrath incurred on the people as a result of their impatience and eventual idolatry (Exodus 32:7-28)?

Historical Insight

Fifteen hundred years ago, a young man studying in Rome became disgusted with the paganism he saw there and decided to live in solitude in a cave some distance outside the city. In that decision Benedict enacted a fantasy that has inflamed the hearts of men and women before and since—the idea of making a life apart from the crowd, in a style at odds with the norm.

One of the great visionaries of the first half millennium of the church is Benedict of Nursia, Italy. He fervently wanted to know how best to live for God within a hostile environment. Benedict looked for solitude in a cave—a retreat location like none other—in order to inquire of the Lord how best to live for Christ in a dark and idolatrous world. Benedict came out of that cave with a treatise—his "Rule of Life"—filled with ideas on how best to live in ways that honor the call of God in the context of prayer and community.

With Benedict we discover the contrast between the spiritual life and the life sought after and encouraged by the world. First, the spiritual life is countercultural. When we walk by the Spirit and seek to fulfill the call of God, we live in a pattern distinctly different from the world around us. What is it about your life in Christ that sets you apart from this world?

Second, the spiritual life is counterintuitive. When we say yes to the call of God, we invite him to reign supreme and take full control over our lives. This runs counter to our human nature, our sinful, self-absorbed natural tendencies. When we embrace a life in the Spirit we are saying to God, "Take over the steering wheel of my life, and I will submit my inclinations to your direction."

Third, the spiritual life often seems counterproductive. In our world, we often are measured by how "productive" or "effective" we can be—in other words, how well we use our time, treasure and talents. We seek the most efficient ways to be productive. We are rewarded and affirmed and often gain our self-esteem by our productivity. For the most part this is good, as is seen in the parable of the talents (Matthew 25).

However, God invites us into an intimate relationship with him, which means we need to regularly say no to productivity and instead "waste" a few productive hours simply attending to God. As we hear the loving, grace-filled voice of God, we leave the fruitfulness of our lives in his hands to accomplish according to his timing, means and grace.

Benedict understood the tension of living by a rule of life that is countercultural, counterintuitive and, yes, even at times counterproductive. Although his rule was written for the monks of his community, it has become a paradigm for others for more than fifteen hundred years. Based on the foundation of humility, obedience and the frugal life, Benedict's rule became a pattern for committed individuals who want more than anything else to live intentionally in the center of God's unique will.

Benedict based his rule on humility. His discourse on humility is centered on the analogy of Jacob's ladder (Genesis 28:10-15) whereby we ascend to heaven by way of humility but descend back to earth by self-exaltation. So, if we discipline and humble our hearts, the Lord will raise us up toward himself. In chapter seven, Benedict describes the twelve steps of humility, which include keeping the fear of God always before our eyes, not satisfying our own desires, living in submission to superiors, being content with lowly acts of service, and control-

ling our tongues and valuing silence.

In his rule Benedict stresses two ideals: community and contemplation.

1. *Community*. Those living out his rule embrace common ownership of property, common worship, common silence, common language, common care for community (authenticity, transparency, reflection), and a communal obedience to Christ, the abbot and to one another. In this community Benedict invites his followers into a posture of humility, particularly as it relates to those in authority and even to a humble embrace of sufferings and failures.

2. *Contemplation*. Those in community share a life of prayer, which includes chanting the Psalms, liturgical music and sacred art; and care for the soul in theology, philosophy, manual labor and social activity. The community gives great attention to reading, develops a keen awareness of the divine presence everywhere and promotes prayerfulness in all spiritual practices.

> Brothers, now that we have asked the Lord who will dwell in his tent, we have heard the instruction for dwelling in it, but only if we fulfill the obligations of those who live there. We must, then, prepare our hearts and bodies for the battle of holy obedience to his instructions. *What is not possible to us by nature, let us ask the Lord to supply by the help of his grace.* If we wish to reach eternal life, even as we avoid the torments of hell, then—while there

is still time, while we are in this body and have time to accomplish all these things by the light of life— we must run and do now what will profit us forever.

Therefore we intend to establish a school for the Lord's service. In drawing up its regulations, we *hope to set down nothing harsh, nothing burdensome.* The good of all concerned, however, may prompt us to a little strictness in order to amend faults and to safeguard love. Do not be daunted immediately by fear and run away from the road that leads to salvation. It is bound to be narrow at the outset. *But as we progress in this way of life and in faith, we shall run on the path of God's commandments, our hearts overflowing with the inexpressible delight of love.* Never swerving from his instructions, then, but faithfully observing his teaching in the monastery until death, we shall through patience share in the sufferings of Christ that we may deserve also to share in his kingdom. Amen.

Seventy-three chapters follow the prologue. With granular specificity these analyze several key areas of life together in community: qualities of the abbot, restraint of speech, praying the divine office at night, singing of psalms during the daily office, handling of serious faults among the brothers, handling private ownership, serving the sick, caring for the elderly, daily manual labor, observance of Lent, reception of guests, letters or gifts for the monks, mutual obedience, and sending brothers on a journey. All of the details for living prayerfully in community are covered in ways that ensure quality of life for all who embrace community life under Benedict's rule.

Benedict exemplifies the fervent pursuit of God's invitation to the well-ordered life. And through the centuries, following his example, many Christians have submitted to his rule or crafted their own rule of life. We are forever indebted to Benedict for this amazing, visionary contribution to the spiritual formation of God's faithful people.

Personal Rule of Life

1. "What is not possible to us by nature, let us ask the Lord to supply by the help of his grace." What aspect of God's grace feels most inviting to you as you consider crafting your own rule of life?

2. "We hope to set down nothing harsh, nothing burdensome." A rule of life is crafted so a full life can be achieved. What do you most fear about writing your own rule that may seem harsh or burdensome?

Moses' vision was to be led by the glory of God, his passion was to see his people set free from bondage and his specific call was to lead them to the Promised Land. Benedict's vision was to create a movement of committed followers of Jesus Christ who shared a life of prayer. His passion was an earnest desire to know God, and his specific call was to invite others into his newly transformed and Christ-centered communal life. In chapter five we will examine our specific mission and purpose. We will explore how our present actions can lead to the fulfillment of our long-term visionary calling.

3. "But as we progress in this way of life and in faith, we shall run on the path of God's commandments, our hearts overflowing with the inexpressible delight of love." How is the path of God's Word coming alive for you in this rule-of-life discovery process?

Our personal rule of life, like Benedict's communal rule, is impossible to fulfill by nature. Though it's not to be harsh or burdensome, it can be accomplished only by the help of God's grace. As we progress in this life by faith, in accordance with God's truth in our hearts, we will overflow with joy. In the prologue to Benedict's Rule, we find three key phrases, which serve as the basis for questions 1-3.

4. *Call.* What has God called you to that only you can fulfill? Without too many specifics, our call is the overarching direction of our life in Christ. It's the way forward toward our vision, and it's fueled by our passion. It's still pretty general when written, and it acknowledges God's hand on our lives for the long haul.

   God has called me to . . .

5. *Passion.* What has God placed deeply in your heart and soul that speaks of your most sincere concern for others and yourself? Passion is the fuel that keeps the engine of your vision alive. It's what God has given to you that few others share in the same way; it comes directly from your life story and feeds into God's invitation to live for his glory. Fill in the blank with words of deep concern: What energizes me the most is my passionate concern for _____.

The passion God has placed deep in my soul is . . .

6. *Vision.* What do you sense God is inviting you to as it relates to your preferred future? It's something attractive that you're running after but have yet to taste. It's "out there" in the future and it's captured your heart like few other things in life. It's that big idea you would like to pursue; prayerfully considering it is exhilarating. Fill in the blank: When I imagine my life in partnership with God, I desire _____ more than anything.

Take time in questions 4-6 to begin writing the following personal rule of life statements. Notice the progression of thought from call to passion to vision. Be open and receptive to the nudging of God's Spirit as you reflect on these questions. Each is designed to help you process the larger, longer-view approach to life and will help you articulate the way forward.

The vision God has planted in my heart for the future can be summarized as follows . . .

Spiritual Community

1. Pray for each member's clarity as it relates to call, passion and vision. Listen to one another's heart on this matter. Where is there anxiety, fear, focus or joy in this process? How can you best come alongside one another in this early stage of the process?

2. Look together at the life of Moses (refer back in this chapter). What about his life was most striking to you and why? How did Moses come to understand his personal rule of life, and how was that fed and fostered by both God and those who surrounded Moses?

3. Regarding their call, passion and vision, what other biblical characters are you drawn to? Explain why.

4. Listen to each other's initial statements of call, passion and vision. As you listen, attend to what the Spirit is saying to and through your friends. Pause before making statements about what you are hearing. Share what you hear each person saying and help your friend identify the longings of his or her heart in these matters. (Try not to offer corrective or comparative advice, and be careful not to shift attention from the person sharing to yourself.)

5. Invite feedback from your friends about what they are hearing from you as you share. Avoid being swayed immediately by their comments, but jot down what they say. Later, take their comments before the Lord as you sit, ponder and pray over God's call, passion and vision on your life. Feel free to revisit these issues as you continue to meet with one another for spiritual friendship and prayerful encouragement.

Be Thou my vision, O Lord of my heart.
Naught be all else to me, save that Thou art.
Thou my best Thought, by day or by night,
Waking or sleeping, Thy presence my light.

Dear Lord, May all that becomes of my vision be to your honor and glory. May my vision for life come from your vision for me, one that's personal, passionate and full of vigor. I long to know your deepest longings for me, and I desire more than anything else to reflect those yearnings to all who cross my path. May it be so in my life and for your glory. In Jesus' name. Amen.

MISSION

What Am I Currently Doing to Pursue My Vision?

Guiding Principle

Mission: **Your personal rule of life is discerned and framed within the specific purpose(s) God invites you to fulfill in this season of life.**

Think back to when you first sensed God's invitation to salvation and you became his adopted and beloved child. What was that experience like for you? Were you slowly formed in Christ since childhood, or were you dramatically called from darkness into light? Jot down a few thoughts here.

Since your recognition of Christ as Lord, when have you sensed an invitation from God to particular areas of service in his kingdom? What was included, and how was this affirmed by others?

> *Are you looking for purpose in life? For a purpose big enough to absorb every ounce of your attention, deep enough to plumb every mystery of your passions, and lasting long enough to inspire you to your last breath? Everything we are, everything we do, and everything we have is invested with a special devotion, dynamism, and direction lived out as a response to his summons and service.*
> —OS GUINNESS

Write a prayer that depicts your heart's deepest yearnings to know and fulfill the mission God invites you to at this season of your life.

Biblical Reflection

I want to know Christ and the power of his resurrection and the fellowship of sharing in his sufferings, becoming like him in his death, and so, somehow, to attain to the resurrection from the dead. . . . Forgetting what is behind and straining toward what is ahead, I press on toward the goal to win the prize for which God has called me heavenward in Christ Jesus. (Philippians 3:10-14)

The apostle Paul is a fabulous example of someone who understood and fulfilled his personal mission. In brief, Paul was an Israelite born in Tarsus, the capital city of Cilicia (Acts 22:3; Philippians 3:5). He was a Roman citizen by birthright (Acts 22:28) and was taught the law by Gamaliel in Jerusalem (Acts 22:3). He was a tentmaker by trade (Acts 18:3) and a devout Pharisee (Philippians 3:5). We know that preconversion, he was present at Stephen's stoning (Acts 7:58; 8:1) and was an avid keeper of the law, one who actively persecuted the church (Acts 9:1-3; Philippians 3:6).

He experienced a dramatic conversion on the way to Damascus (Acts 9:1-9), after which he went to the wilderness of Arabia (Galatians 1:17), where his new character was formed in Christ. He traveled to many cities preaching the gospel to both Jews and Gentiles (book of Acts). He was imprisoned several times for preaching the gospel (Colossians 4:10; 2 Timothy 1:8) Finally, he was sent as prisoner to Rome (Acts 27:1; 28:16). Tradition tells us he was eventually martyred.

Paul wrote many letters to the churches, exhorting them to walk worthy of their calling and to remain faithful to the gospel that he brought to them. In total, thirteen of his letters are included in the New Testament, including letters written to Christian communities in Rome, Corinth, Galatia, Ephesus, Philippi, Colossae and Thessalonica. He also addressed letters to several Christian leaders: Timothy, Titus and Philemon.

From the time of his dramatic conversion on the road to Damascus (Acts 9), Paul was transformed into a man on a mission from God. A startling light thrust him to the ground and temporarily blinded him. He was illumined by a vision, confirmed in his baptism and directed on a mission: preach to the Gentiles, proclaiming Jesus as the Son of God. He turned his back on his previous mission of persecuting the church and began a new mission of building the church. He is forever known as the central figure of the early church, and his impact continues to bear unprecedented fruit.

For the apostle Paul, discerning the way forward came directly and dramatically from God. The startling bright light that threw him to the ground and blinded his eyes was about as obvious as it comes. Some have had equally remarkable experiences.

For others, however, the movement of the Spirit may be almost indistinguishable—the polar opposite of what Paul experienced. The only option is to pray for the Spirit to take the lead, without which there is no discernment whatsoever.

Here, discerning the will and mission of God is more challenging because it requires prayerful consideration, weighing options and making choices. Often clarity is attained through prayerful discernment between one or more options for the journey that lies ahead.

> Discernment at its best is the consequence of a daily and lifetime walk with God. A lifetime of such companionship produces profound results that range from guidance in decision making to transformation of one's life. Living a life of discernment, then, is a simple process of staying attentive to and open to God in all of the active and contemplative times of our lives.

Discernment begins with distinguishing the presence and empowerment of God. It also requires determining to move out of indecision, immobility or lack of clarity. In discerning among options it's essential that a thoughtful, prayerful, deliberate process unfold one step at a time.

This begins with attentiveness to all potential pathways and destinations. Each needs to be fully explored. The next step, once all are listed, is to weigh each option individually, with openness and transparency about the positives and negatives of each. Holding each as lightly as possible, prayerfully considering the negatives (yes, start with the why *not*s), followed by the positives for each. One by one the poorer alternatives will eventually be eliminated. This will lead you to the one best option, which should be held up to multifaceted scrutiny before the final decision is made. Once determined, the discernment process closes and movement forward commences. (For more on spiritual discernment, go to www.leadershiptransformations.org/offer.htm.)

This is why the apostle Paul was so deliberate in his prayers for those he served. He presented the gospel with conviction, and the principles of a godly life were made crystal clear, but the application for each church was different. Paul prayed for their discernment and direction, and gave them the freedom to follow the Spirit according to their particular needs and situation as they fulfilled their mission from God.

Paul's mission included his deliberate life of prayer. In his epistles we see Paul, led in the fullness of the Spirit, expressing profound prayers for the churches and individuals he served. We will linger here for a while as we contemplate our own personal mission. How are the prayers of Paul an aid to the discovery of our own personal mission today? How are the prayers of the saints being fulfilled in us as members of the body of Christ?

Let's take a look at some of Paul's prayers for the churches.

Paul prays for wisdom and revelation that the eyes of their heart may be enlightened:

I keep asking that the God of our Lord Jesus Christ, the glorious Father, may give you the Spirit of *wisdom and revelation*, so that you may know him better. I pray also that the *eyes of your heart may be enlightened* in order that you may know the hope to which he has called you, the riches of his glorious inheritance in the saints, and his incomparably great power for us who believe. (Ephesians 1:17-23, emphasis added)

Paul wants Christians to fully comprehend the love of Christ:

I pray that you, being rooted and established in love, may have power, together with all the saints, to *grasp how wide and long and high and deep is the love of Christ, and to know this love that surpasses knowledge—that you may be filled to the measure of all the fullness of God.*

Now to him who is able to do immeasurably more than all we ask or imagine, according to his power that is at work within us, to him be glory in the church and in Christ Jesus throughout all generations, forever and ever! Amen. (Ephesians 3:17-21, emphasis added)

Paul also prays for their depth of insight, that they may be able to discern what's best in life and ministry:

And this is my prayer: that your *love may abound more and more in knowledge and depth of insight, so that you*

may be able to discern what is best and may be pure and blameless until the day of Christ, filled with the fruit of righteousness that comes through Jesus Christ—to the glory and praise of God. (Philippians 1:9-11, emphasis added)

Additionally, Paul prays for God to fill his people with knowledge, wisdom and understanding:

For this reason, since the day we heard about you, we have not stopped praying for you and asking God to fill you with the *knowledge of his will through all spiritual wisdom and understanding.* And we pray this in order that you may live a life worthy of the Lord and may please him in every way: bearing fruit in every good work, growing in the knowledge of God, being strengthened with all power according to his glorious might so that you may have great endurance and patience, and joyfully giving thanks to the Father, who has qualified you to share in the inheritance of the saints in the kingdom of light. (Colossians 1:9-12, emphasis added)

And Paul prays for faith, love and hope:

We continually remember before our God and Father your *work produced by faith, your labor prompted by love, and your endurance inspired by hope* in our Lord Jesus Christ. (1 Thessalonians 1:3, emphasis added)

In spiritual discernment we are seeking a growing awareness to two important matters: (1) God's invitation to come close, draw near and follow him to a place of intimacy and companionship, and (2) God's intention to fulfill his will for our lives on a daily basis and throughout our lifetime. May we all learn from Paul, who prayed that through wisdom, discernment and power from on high we might capture greater clarity of our own personal mission.

Discernment for the Christian community begins with the individual Christian. Do I want to know God's will more than anything else? This question is the entryway into discernment. And it can be answered with affirmation only by those who love God and have learned to trust God. If we have any higher priority in our search for God's guidance, we will not be able to trust our discernment. I must spend enough time in prayer and faithful listening to the voice of God to be brought to that moment of trust and surrender when I can give up my preconceived ideas and become open to God's idea. Can Christians know God's will? Can the Church know God's will? Can our congregation know God's will? Nearly two thousand years of experience shout a resounding yes!

1. Paul's vision was to call people from among the Gentiles to faith in and obedience to Jesus Christ our Lord (Romans 1:5). This ultimately led to his mission to Rome and Spain (see Romans 15:24). Read Galatians 1:11-17—what was revealed to Paul, and what do you see here that describes his personal mission?

2. Read Ephesians 3:1-21. Here Paul describes his specific mission to preach to the Gentiles the unsearchable riches of Christ. What are the "riches" Paul is referring to, and how are they revealed in his prayer for the Ephesians?

3. Read Philippians 3:1-11 and Colossians 1:24–2:5 and jot down phrases that could serve as Paul's personal mission statement. Circle key words that strike a responsive chord within you and could be applied to your own mission.

Historical Insight

Adoniram Judson, the first missionary sent from America, knew his mission with great clarity. His *roles* were leader, pioneer, husband, missionary and friend. His *gifts* were evangelism and linguistics. His *desire* was to be the first American missionary sent internationally. His *vision* was to spread the gospel around the world, but specifically to Burma. His *mission* was to devote his life and energy to presenting the gospel to the Burmese people, giving them the Word of God in their own language, and developing a dictionary for others to continue the work after his death.

Adoniram was born August 9, 1788, in Malden, Massachusetts, to the Reverend Adoniram Judson Sr. and his wife Abigail Brown Judson. At a young age it was evident he was very bright. In grammar school his reputation for mathematics had extended into language—Greek and Latin—and his schoolmates called him Virgil.

In 1804, days after turning sixteen, Adoniram entered the Rhode Island College at Providence (now Brown University). He was so far along in the subjects of Latin, Greek, mathematics, geography, astronomy, logic, oratory, rhetoric and moral philosophy that he was able to skip the freshman coursework and enter as a sophomore. He became very close friends with Jacob Eames, a deist. His friendship with Eames led to the collapse of the faith he grew up with. At nineteen, Judson graduated as valedictorian of his class. He subsequently was a school

teacher and wrote textbooks. On his twentieth birthday Adoniram broke the news to his parents that their God was not his God. He revealed that he had become a deist and wanted to go to New York to try his luck in writing plays. His parents were heartbroken. His time in New York was short lived.

Rather than head home from New York, Adoniram went to visit his uncle Ephraim. Ephraim was away, but a young minister was staying in his stead. Adoniram and the minister spent several hours in conversation, and Judson was thoroughly impressed. The next day he left his uncle's house and stopped at a small village inn for night's lodging. The inn was almost full to capacity—the only room left was next to a young man on his deathbed. Throughout the night Judson heard the man groan and moan. Upon leaving the inn, Judson asked the innkeeper how the young man was. The innkeeper informed him that he was dead. Judson asked who he was. The innkeeper responded, "Young man from college in Providence. Name was Eames. Jacob Eames."

This revelation shocked Adoniram, and he departed for home almost immediately. He did not know exactly what was happening but believed God was up to something; he feared for his soul. In the fall of 1808 Adoniram enrolled in Andover Theological Seminary. Without a declaration of religious belief he was not a candidate for ministry but was a special student. As with college he skipped the first year of studies because of his academic achievements. With a natural propensity for languages, he began studying the Scriptures in their original languages.

On December 2, 1808, Judson dedicated himself to God. This may in fact be considered his conversion. From this time on he was literally a new man. He banished forever his ambitions of worldly success and simply asked himself, "How shall I so order my future being as best to please God?" In September 1809 Adoniram read a sermon titled "The Star in the East," about missions to the eastern hemisphere, and the seed was planted for his desire to become the first missionary sent from North America. But there was no organization that could send and support foreign missionaries.

All at once his imagination kindled. An amazing, a brilliant, a dazzling prospect appeared to him. Why should not *he* be a foreign missionary to one of these remote parts of the world as yet unreached by the Gospel? He would be the first Congregational foreign missionary—the first American, the very first! Everything in his life had prepared him for the idea. A career as the first American foreign missionary curiously combined his many conflicting ambitions. Fame, eminence, humility, self-sacrifice, obscurity, adventure, uniqueness, the service of God.

Judson's aptitude for languages supported his idea of becoming a missionary because missionaries needed to translate the Bible into the mother tongue of the peoples being evangelized. Judson set his sights on the Burmese people. On one cold day in February 1810,

during a solitary walk in the woods behind the college, while meditating and praying on the subject, and feeling half inclined to give it up, that the command of Christ, "Go into all the world and preach the Gospel to every creature," was presented to my mind with such clearness and power, that I came to a full decision, and though great difficulties appeared in my way, resolved to obey the command at all events.

Four months later, on June 28, 1810, Judson and several others submitted themselves to the Congregationalists for an endorsement and support for missions to the East. This is also the day Judson met his first wife, Anne Hasseltine (who went by Nancy).

Barely a month after meeting Nancy, Judson was convinced that he wanted to marry her. So he wrote the following letter to Nancy's father, Deacon John Hasseltine.

I have now to ask, whether you can consent to part with your daughter early next spring, to see her no more in this world; whether you can consent to her departure, and her subjection to the hardships and sufferings of a missionary life; whether you can consent to her exposure to the dangers of the ocean; to the fatal influence of the southern climate of

India; to every kind of want and distress; to degradation, insult, persecution, and perhaps a violent death. Can you consent to all this, for the sake of him who left his heavenly home, and died for her and for you; for the sake of perishing immortal souls; for the sake of Zion, and the glory of God?

Adoniram and Nancy were married February 5, 1812, and less than two weeks later they were aboard the *Caravan*, sailing to India. By the summer of 1813 they had arrived at Rangoon, Burma, and began a lifelong battle with cholera, malaria, dysentery and unknown miseries that would eventually take two of Judson's wives, seven of his thirteen children, and colleague after colleague in death.

Judson devoted himself to translating the Scriptures into Burmese as well as to writing gospel tracts. Six years after arriving in Burma, God provided the first convert, Maung Nau. In response to this conversion Adoniram wrote, "It seems almost too much to believe that God has begun to manifest his grace to the Burmans; but this day I could not resist the delightful conviction that this is really the case. PRAISE AND GLORY BE TO HIS NAME FOREVER MORE. Amen." There was a glimmer of hope that years of hard work were finally paying off, but the work remained difficult.

In May 1824 the British fleets attacked Rangoon's harbor. The Burmese suspected that every foreigner was a spy. By June 1824 Adoniram was thrown into prison. In order to protect the only Burmese New Testament translation in existence, Nancy brought Adoniram the manuscript stuffed inside a pillow so he could keep an eye on it. November 1825 he was released from prison because the Burmese government required his bilingual talents in their negotiations with the British. One year later Nancy died, and in the spring of 1827 their baby girl died.

By the grace of God in 1831 the desire for Bible tracts skyrocketed. Everyone in Burma seemed to want to learn about the new gospel. Adoniram had to write more tracts and suggested the printing of another edition. The missionaries were giving away hundreds of tracts every day.

On April 6, 1834, Adoniram married Sarah H. Boardman, whose husband died on the mission field in Burma. Judson and Sarah had eight children. On October 24, 1840, Adoniram sent the final sheets of the complete Burmese Bible to the printing house. Once this mammoth task was finished he set his sights on creating an English-Burmese dictionary. In 1845 Sarah died while traveling to America for medical help.

While back in America, Judson, now fifty-seven, married twenty-nine-year-old Emily Chubbuck, in June 1846. They returned to Burma, and Adoniram continued working on the dictionary, overseeing the work of the mission, and preaching on Sundays. On January 24, 1849, Judson completed the six-hundred-page English-Burmese section of the dictionary. At the beginning of 1850 Adoniram became so sick that he had to put off working on the second part (the Burmese-English section).

While traveling aboard the *Aristide* *Marie* to seek medical help in America, Adoniram died on April 12, 1850. He was sixty-one and had devoted almost forty years on mission to the Burmese people.

Personal Rule of Life

1. List words and phrases that best describe your current areas of involvement—your major areas of relationship and responsibility at home, work, school, ministry and church. Prayerfully review this list to be sure it's accurate and comprehensive.

> *With the backdrop of roles, gifts, passions and vision before us, now is the time to ponder the subject of mission. As you answer questions 1-3, ask, What is God inviting me to consider as my personal mission? This foundational question completes the framework of your rule of life and clarifies what you invest in as a child of God, set apart for purposes greater than yourself.*

2. Which of these relationships and responsibilities need even greater attention today? Explain.

3. If given the opportunity, which of these relationships and responsibilities could you eliminate or hold off from attending to during this season of your life? Why?

4. What relationships do you feel called by God to deepen in the coming weeks and months?

5. What responsibilities do you feel called by God to strengthen in the coming weeks and months?

6. Prayerfully consider writing a draft of your personal mission statement. After writing it here, read it several times and share it with a friend. Edit and revise accordingly.

> *As you answer questions 4-6, consider your current and preferred mission and purpose in life, prayerfully pondering both the "doing" and "being" that embody your daily service to others. Building on what you've discovered in previous chapters, what is God inviting you to consider as you discern this central aspect of your personal rule of life?*

Spiritual Community

1. What in the life of the apostle Paul most energizes or encourages you as you formulate your own personal mission statement?

2. What in the life of Adoniram Judson excites you to become more focused on discerning your personal mission?

3. What aspect of spiritual discernment are you most intrigued by and desire to learn more about? (Consider prayerfully reviewing Rueben Job's *Guide to Spiritual Discernment*, Gordon T. Smith's *The Voice of Jesus* or some of the other resources on spiritual discernment available on Leadership Transformations' online store, www. LeadershipTransformations.org/store.)

4. What was it like for you to work on defining your current relationships and responsibilities in light of defining your personal mission statement? How did the outcome

(a draft of your statement) help you focus on God's invitation for you during this season of your life?

5. If you are willing, share your personal mission statement with members of your group. Celebrate together the clarity that has been achieved through this process. Pray for one another and ask the Lord to confirm or provide additional clarity for each member of the group. Remember that all of this is a work in progress (as are we).

Lord Jesus, may I be captivated today by your Great Commission, to go into all the world and preach the gospel, inviting others to become disciples of yours now and forever. May your mission become my own, for I long to know how best to reflect that in my daily life and service to others in your name. Whisper in my ear and continually invite me into deeper fellowship with you, which will result in a life of mission with you and co-mission with others. Illuminate the path and enlighten my heart so that I may be refreshed and renewed in all my ways. In Christ's name and for his glorious sake I pray. Amen.

Personal Rule of Life Statements

Your personal rule of life is a holistic description of the Spirit-empowered rhythms and relationships that create, redeem, sustain and transform the life God invites you to humbly fulfill for Christ's glory.

In order to begin to frame your rule of life (the focus of our first five chapters), we've covered five very important issues: roles, gifts, desires, vision and mission. Each of these areas needs to be clarified as best as possible so that the general overview of your life is clearly understood and articulated as you move forward in crafting a personal rule of life. Before moving on to part two, look back over the previous five chapters and summarize your thoughts here. How is the Lord leading you in all five of these overarching arenas of your personal life? Record your thoughts below.

My Roles:

My Gifts:

My Desires:

My Vision:

My Mission:

PART TWO

Forming Your Personal Rule of Life

Christ be with me, Christ within me,
Christ behind me, Christ before me,
Christ beside me, Christ to win me,
Christ to comfort and restore me.
Christ beneath me, Christ above me,
Christ in quiet, Christ in danger,
Christ in hearts of all that love me,
Christ in mouth of friend and stranger.

FROM ST. PATRICK'S BREASTPLATE

6

TIME

Spiritual Priorities

Guiding Principle

Time: **Your personal rule of life is formed and reflected in your daily, weekly, monthly, quarterly and annual spiritual rhythms and practices.**

Think back over the past twenty-four hours. What occupied the majority of your time? Reflect on the past week. Which relationships and responsibilities dominated your schedule? Where, when and how in your past day or week did God emerge as your priority?

If you could re-create your past twenty-four hours, what would you like to do differently: Reconstruct a conversation? Reorder a priority? Renew a relationship or responsibility? Add a particular discipline?

> *Divine Majesty.*
> *Oh Blessed Indulgence! Oh most Happy Day!*
>
> *Lord I can never sufficiently adore Thy*
>   *Infinite Love and Goodness*
> *in approaching this uninterrupted part of my*
>   *time to Thy Self.*
> *May these sacred moments ever be employed*
>   *in Thy service.*
> *May no vain unnecessary or unprofitable*
>   *thoughts or discourse ever rob You of Your*
>   *due honour and praise on this Day;*
> *or deprive my soul of the peculiar advantages*
> *and blessings which are to be gained,*
> *by the conscientious performance of the*
>   *duties of the Day.*
> —SUSANNA WESLEY, "THIS IS THE DAY"

What about in the past week? Where did you sense order versus disorder, fullness versus emptiness, time well spent versus time wasted, consolation versus desolation?

Where, when and how was God tapping you on the shoulder of your heart but you might have missed his loving initiatives because you were too busy or distracted to listen?

Biblical Reflection

When you pray, go into your room, close the door and pray to your Father, who is unseen. Then your Father, who sees what is done in secret, will reward you. (Matthew 6:6)

From the earliest days of Christian history, believers have developed ways of structuring our use of time to reflect our most fundamental beliefs and to commemorate our most meaningful historical events.

The Christian year is built around this calendar of events starting with Advent and Christmas, followed by Epiphany, Lent and Easter, with Pentecost, and then Ordinary Time, which lead back into harvest and All Saints' Day. We go full circle and arrive back at Advent where the calendar repeats itself once more. The rhythm of the seasons in each year helps us to remember with thanksgiving the ongoing, well-ordered and redemptive work of Christ.

The Christian week focuses on the blessings and joys of creation, when after six days of work, the Lord ceased from his labors and embraced sabbath rest. Setting apart one day each week, God modeled for his children how he wants us to live. He wants us to work faithfully for six days and then rest deeply for one. That rhythm is the most life-sustaining of all and will keep us from burning out on too much work, by far the most damaging temptation of seeking to live fully today. Choosing sabbath as a slow down, rest, delight, notice and be fulfilled lifestyle will lead us into the abundant life Christ invites us to embrace and enjoy.

For the Christian even a day in itself is to be seen as holy. The church fathers and mothers practiced their life of prayer and devotion throughout their days. Known as the "hours" (liturgy of the hours or book of hours) or the "office" (divine or daily office), these are the seven points in the day that are markers of holiness. Based on Psalm 119:164, "Seven times a day I praise you for your righteous laws," the daily office sets apart holy moments in the day to pause, reflect and remember our source of life (*matins* in the morning; *vespers* in the evening; *terce*, *sext* and *none*, the third, sixth and ninth hours of midday; *compline* just before bed; and *prime* for the very early morning). It was first practiced in early monastic communities, and the daily office is still followed today in Roman Catholic, Orthodox, Anglican, Lutheran and

Reformed churches (although not exactly alike). These holy times of the day are worth our consideration regardless of our Christian tradition. For evangelicals, this expands the "daily quiet time" from one set time each day to several prayers and pauses throughout the day. Can we argue with such value for the soul?

In addition to the church calendar, the Christian week and the daily office, our faith tradition honors the importance of holy spaces (with corresponding biblical theologies of space and architecture) and holy places (Jerusalem, Rome, Canterbury or Santiago).

All in all, time and space have been important priorities for Christians throughout church history. The use of time and space to aid us in our spiritual development is not a new concept. Neither is our abuse and neglect of both. Therefore, there is a desperate need for us to use our time for the specific growth and development of our spiritual lives— the care and nurture of our souls.

Time is our most basic and often the most precious currency we have. Once spent it's gone forever, except for the memories. As the wisdom of Solomon teaches us in Ecclesiastes 3:1, "There is a time for everything, and a season for every activity under heaven." Likewise, David reminds us in Psalm 31:15, "My times are in your hands." As with them, it is true for us: There is a time for everything under heaven, and our times are in God's hands.

Creating space for God is the number one discipline of the soul, and the best place to do that is in our devotional prayer closet (in addition to and complementary of the time we share with God's people in worship and prayer as a faith community). Do you have a personal place and time set apart to meet alone with God? You might practice the daily office and set apart seven times each day to enter this space, but at minimum Christ's followers should set apart at least one part of every day for this purpose. Known as a quiet time or daily devotions, this establishes a rhythm of place and time to attend to the loving embrace and tender voice of almighty God.

Here, we say no to all worldly intrusions in order to say yes to all that God delights to offer, including his love, grace, mercy, peace, joy, strength, wisdom, direction, pleasure, presence and ongoing empowerment. In this set apart time and space we reorder our loves and reorient our lives around God-honoring priorities. When we press the pause button and stop long enough to enter and enjoy his loving embrace, we receive more and more of God. As Mark Buchanan reminds us, as we rest in God, we discover the rest of God:

> Most of us feel utterly ransacked. We are waylaid by endless demands and stifling routines. Even our vacations have a panicky, task-like edge to them. "If I only had more time," is the mantra of our age. But is this the real problem? What we've really lost is "the rest of God—the rest God bestows and, with it, that part of himself" we can know only through stillness.

So Jesus inquires of his disciples,

> Are you tired? Worn out? Burned out on religion? Come to me. Get away with me and you'll recover your life. I'll show you how to take a real rest. Walk with me and work with me— watch how I do it. Learn the unforced rhythms of grace. I won't lay anything heavy or ill-fitting on you. Keep company with me and you'll learn to live freely and lightly. (Matthew 11:28-30 *The Message*)

Learning the unforced rhythms of grace requires practice. We're prone to meeting the demands of the busy life. We wake up each day and maximize every moment before us: getting ready as fast as possible, eating a quick breakfast before running out the door, packing every possible moment with meetings, work, chores, children, exercise, driving, shopping, eating, e-mails, phone calls, errands, ministry, just to name a few. Yes, our lives are stretched to the maximum; our days are full from the time we awaken to the time we drop into bed. And though we're living very full days, we often come to the realization that in fact we're quite unfulfilled because there's no time to simply *be*.

Twentieth-century spiritual formation author Evelyn Underhill says it this way:

> We mostly spend our lives conjugating three verbs: to Want, to Have, and to Do. Craving, clutching, and fussing, on the material, political, social, emotional, intellectual— even the religious—plane, we are kept in perpetual unrest: forgetting that none of these verbs have any ultimate significance, except so far as they are transcended by and included in, the fundamental verb, to Be: and that Being, not wanting, not having and not doing, is the essence of a spiritual life.

It sounds to me like she understands the heart of learning the unforced rhythms of grace.

Where do we learn these unforced rhythms of grace? In our prayer closets, where we slow down long enough to enter into this open, uncluttered space at an unhurried pace, and where we *learn to do nothing well*. It's here where we discover the true values and sweet virtues of silence and solitude. Time alone with God that's life-giving, life-sustaining, life-redeeming and life-transforming.

The key is *unhurried, uncluttered, unhindered space*—experienced in our prayer closets so we can enter the world with a fuller sense of God's abiding presence and peace, which guide and sustain us every step of the way. Our prayer closets are set-apart spaces within the bounds of our home environment (or another quiet location). This set-apart time and space is enhanced by the beauty and joy of God's creation, like enjoying the expanse of the sky, water, mountains, trees, birds, animals and all that he provides for us to savor with all of our senses. It is deepened all the more when we're together with our spiritual family (our local believing community) in regular times of worship, prayer, study, confession, thanksgiving and consecration.

What happens in our prayer closet? We practice the threefold disciplines of Scripture reading (receiving the Word of God into the good soil of our soul), prayer (conversing honestly with and listening attentively to God) and reflection (in the pages of our journals or other ways of collecting the experiences of life and learning from them). These are the three basic nutrients of the spiritual life. The Word, our source of life, is received as food to nourish and replenish our tired and weary souls. In prayer we welcome the voice of the Father as he whispers truth, love and counsel into our daily existence. With reflection, we pause to remember and give thanks for the gifts that life has to offer us, as we look around and within to determine the best ways to move forward in sharing these with others.

There are many options for each of these basic disciplines. A wonderful resource for exploring them in depth is Adele Calhoun's *Spiritual Disciplines Handbook*, in which you will be invited into silence and solitude, submission and surrender, confession and forgiveness, listening and interactive prayer—soaking in the joy of intimacy with Christ.

As we discover afresh the joy of an ever-deepening devotional experience, the gift of new life is brought to our souls. Out of this sacred space, we enter into community worship and shared witness with vitality that's contagious—both to the body of Christ and the world we've been called to serve together in Jesus' name.

Those who traveled with Jesus watched him regularly create time and space to be alone and quiet before the Father. This was an obvious priority for him. His disciples were all privy to these ongoing times of prayer and reflection. "Jesus often withdrew to lonely places and prayed" (Luke 5:16). "Very early in the morning, while it was still dark, Jesus got up, left the house and went off to a solitary place, where he prayed" (Mark 1:35).

The beloved disciple of the Gospel of John, who many believe was the apostle John, drew near to Jesus on multiple occasions. He remains a stark contrast to Judas the Betrayer, the disciple who turned away from Jesus and continually rejected Jesus' initiatives to come close, draw near and follow him (cf. John 13; 18).

The Gospel of John in particular outlines the times when we see with clarity the cherished relationship between Jesus and the beloved disciple:

- At the Last Supper John reclined close to Jesus (John 13:23-26).

- At the cross, Jesus entrusts his mother to him (John 19:25-27).

- John runs with Peter to the open tomb and believes (John 20:1-10).

- He recognizes the Lord after his resurrection (John 21:4-7).

- He follows Peter and Jesus at a close distance (John 21:20-23).

- He's an eyewitness source of the Gospel of John (John 21:24).

All of these snapshots show us the intimacy of fellowship enjoyed by Jesus and his beloved disciple. They provide an inspiration to all who follow in his footsteps toward an ever-deepening walk with Christ.

What about for you, a devoted disciple who longs for intimacy with Christ and being known fully as his beloved disciple? Will you take the time to create the space to meet with the lover of your soul and the giver of your life? The richest fellowship with Jesus is most accessible at his feet or reclining at table with him. The invitation to the beloved is also offered to you, his dearly loved child. Come close, draw near and follow him with a well-ordered and properly reordered heart. "Come with me by yourselves to a quiet place and get some rest" (Mark 6:31).

1. At the Last Supper, "the disciple whom Jesus loved" (John 13:23) was reclining next to Jesus. Imagine for a few moments being the beloved disciple. What's going through your mind as you reflect upon the foot washing and Last Supper experiences (John 13)? As you linger in this passage, how will you posture yourself to receive the "full extent of his love" today?

2. At the cross, Jesus entrusts his mother to the beloved disciple (John 19). What does this tell you about Jesus' relationships with his mother and his closest companion? From what you know about the Gospels, what memories might Mary and the beloved disciple be reflecting on as they look back on their years on earth with Jesus?

3. At the empty tomb the beloved disciple stands with Peter in utter amazement and astonished belief (John 20). He is risen indeed! What is it about the truth of the resurrection that brings forth life and renewal within your soul? If our new life in Christ is settled forever in the resurrection of Jesus from the dead, how does this affect your intimacy with God and your testimony of his greatness and power?

Historical Insight

By far one of church's greatest theologians is Jonathan Edwards. Born in 1703, he was the only son of Timothy Edwards, a pastor, and Esther Stoddard Edwards, who had eleven children. His grandfather was Solomon Stoddard, a famous Northampton, Massachusetts, pastor. Edwards's daily priorities included the diligent care of his heart and soul.

Edwards attended Yale College at the age of thirteen, much earlier than most of his contemporaries. After graduation, he pastored a small Presbyterian church in New York City. He then returned to Yale to become a tutor. In his early twenties, he struggled with depression, social awkwardness and a lack of career prospects. He even started believing he was not one of the "elect," according to the Puritan conception of salvation.

However, he had a mystical experience that led him to believe he was regenerated by the Spirit—he wrote that his full conversion suddenly led him to embrace the concept of predestination and the beauty of God's sovereignty. In 1727, he took over pastoral duties from his grandfather, Solomon Stoddard, in Northampton and married Sarah Pierpont. In 1733 the Great Awakening flared and emanated out of Northampton.

While Edwards downplayed the physical and mystical outbursts during the revival, he nevertheless defended their presence since he believed the Spirit was working through them to bring about a great moral improvement in New England. His prayer and devotional life informed his thinking and practices, both in the pulpit and in his extensive writings.

During the first burst of revival, Edwards's name became known to ministers in Scotland and England, and he began a professional acquaintance with the British revival preacher George Whitefield. Toward the tail end of the revival, he wrote his *Religious Affections* in order to establish a balanced, moderate view of the revival. His sermons remain famous today, including such titles as "Sinners in the Hands of an Angry God," which depicts the agonies of those who do not plead for God's forgiveness. (Those who heard this message responded not only in repentance but with leaping shouts of joy.) Most of Edwards's messages, however, focused on the unconditional love of God.

Jonathan Edwards was nearly obsessed with the pursuit of holiness. It consumed him over his lifetime—literally. He ate and drank little, since he was worried about making "fleshly" idols; people often commented on his gaunt, skeletal frame. According to an early biographical source, Edwards spent thirteen hours a day in his study, reading, writing and meeting parishioners. (He refused to do home visits, unlike his affable grandfather—one reason he was later booted from the parish.)

How does the life-transforming power of God's love affect the heart inclined in his direction? From his writings we can see his powerful insights and intentions:

> True religion, in great part, consists in holy affections.
>
> It may be inquired, what the affections of the mind are? I answer, the affections are no other, than the more vigorous and sensible exercises of the inclination and will of the soul.
>
> True religion consists, in a great measure, in vigorous and lively acting on the inclination and will of the soul, or the fervent exercises of the heart.
>
> True religion is evermore a powerful thing; and the power of it appears, in the first place, in the inward exercises of it in the heart, where is the principal and original seat of it.
>
> The affections are very much the spring of men's actions, this also shows, that true religion must consist very much in the affections.
>
> I am bold to assert, that there never was any considerable change wrought in the mind or conversation of any one person, by anything of a religious nature, that ever he read, heard or saw, that had not his affections moved.
>
> But yet it is evident, that religion consists so much in affection, as that without holy affection there is no true religion: and no light in the understanding is good, which don't produce holy affection in the heart.

Demonstrating Edwards's early obsession with holiness and the devotional life, he continuously wrote and updated his now famous "Resolutions"—a document he crafted over time and kept adding to as his life in Christ matured, and the additions are dated accordingly. The fullness and richness of his text inspires some and intimidates others. However, reading his "Resolutions" challenges all of us to consider the significance and priority of our own personal prayer closet and pursuit of a regular devotional expression.

> Being sensible that I am unable to do anything without God's help, I do humbly entreat him, by his grace, to enable me to keep these Resolutions, so far as they are agreeable to his will, for Christ's sake.
>
> 1. Resolved, That I will do whatsoever I think to be most to the glory of God, and my own good, profit, and pleasure, in the whole of my duration; without any consideration of the time, whether now, or never so many myriads of ages hence. Resolved, to do whatever I think to be my duty, and most for the good and advantage of mankind in general. Resolved, so to do, whatever difficulties I meet with, how many soever, and how great soever.
>
> 4. Resolved, Never to do any manner of thing, whether in soul or body, less or more, but what tends to the glory of God, nor be, nor suffer it, if I can possibly avoid it.
>
> 5. Resolved, Never to lose one moment of time, but to improve it in the most profitable way I possibly can.

6. Resolved, To live with all my might, while I do live.

18. Resolved, To live so, at all times, as I think is best in my most devout frames, and when I have the clearest notions of the things of the gospel, and another world.

25. Resolved, To examine carefully and constantly, what that one thing in me is, which causes me in the least to doubt of the love of God; and so direct all my forces against it.

28. Resolved, To study the Scriptures so steadily, constantly, and frequently, as that I may find, and plainly perceive, myself to grow in the knowledge of the same.

30. Resolved, To strive every week to be brought higher in religion, and to a higher exercise of grace, than I was the week before.

37. Resolved, To inquire every night, as I am going to bed, wherein I have been negligent,—what sin I have committed,—and wherein I have denied myself;—also, at the end of every week, month, and year.

48. Resolved, Constantly, with the utmost niceness and diligence, and the strictest scrutiny, to be looking into the state of my soul, that I may know whether I have truly an interest in Christ or not; that when I come to die, I may not have any negligence respecting this to repent of.

The remarkable life of Jonathan Edwards points future generations of serious Christians toward establishing their own particular priorities of the spiritual life. Edwards's example is quite rare and unique, and certainly not a model every Christian can follow. However, he inspires us to examine our heart and to align it with God's unique priorities for the church. Edwards practiced what he preached and serves as an example of deep commitment to the care of the soul. What will be your response and how will his example help you to reorder your own love for God?

Personal Rule of Life

1. What is your current spiritual practice in relation to the Word of God? How are you reading and reflecting on the biblical text?

2. What is your current spiritual practice in relation to your life of prayer? How do you define prayer and in what ways are you continuing to learn how to pray?

3. What is your current spiritual practice in relation to being reflective about your life, relationships, ministry to others and service in the marketplace, community and so on? If you are using a journal to record these reflections, how is this enhancing this spiritual practice? If you are not journaling, how else are you leaning into reflection as a spiritual practice?

The granularity of one's rule of life begins with the spiritual priorities of the soul. With your own plan for personal piety in mind, what are the practices that feed your heart with more of God—particularly in your prayer closet? How and where will you focus on the disciplines of sabbath, silence and solitude, reading Scripture, developing a life of prayer, and the ongoing rhythms of reflection? Questions 1-3 will help you unwrap this concept one morsel at a time. Pay attention along the way to the nudging of the Spirit as he invites you into deeper fellowship with him.

4. What words or phrases best describe the state of your heart and soul today? What words or phrases best describe your desired state of heart and soul (your relationship with God the Father, Son and Holy Spirit)?

After answering questions 4-6, take time to begin writing the following personal rule of life statements listed on page 91.

5. What is the current condition of your "prayer closet"? A center of quiet is best achieved within a space that's conducive for uninterrupted time to read, reflect and receive the Word of God; enter into prayerful communion with the Lord; and practice the discipline of reflection. How can you carve out time and space for this priority to be enhanced in the future?

6. Beyond your personal "prayer closet" experience, in order to practice sabbath rest (as a day set apart as well as a lifestyle) what kind of help do you need to deepen and strengthen your walk with God today and into the future? In the following chart, list the people, places and events that emerge as priorities which contribute to the deepening of your relationship with God.

TIME: YOUR SPIRITUAL PRIORITIES	
Daily/regularly	
Weekly	
Monthly	
Quarterly/seasonally	
Annually	

Spiritual Community

1. What do you most appreciate about the intimate relationship between Jesus and the beloved disciple? What is it about their relationship that you desire with Jesus today?

2. Jonathan Edwards zealously maintained his spiritual intimacy with Christ. He inspires some and intimidates others. Where do you fit on this spectrum? In what ways is God inviting you to deepen your intimacy with him during this season of your life?

3. How does quality space and time (or lack thereof) devoted to deepening intimacy with Christ affect your relationships with others, even within your circle of spiritual friends?

4. What is the current state of your soul, and in what ways are you longing for a deeper walk with God? Specify how you would like to relate to Scripture, listen for God's voice in prayer, and reflect on the highs and lows of daily life.

5. Discuss how each of you are seeking to enhance your personal prayer-closet experience—preserving space and time alone with God as unhurried, unhindered and uncluttered. If you are willing, show your group what your "Time: Your Spiritual Priorities" column looks like.

> *O God, heavenly Father, whose Son Jesus Christ enjoyed rest and refreshment in the home of Mary and Martha of Bethany: Give us the will to love you, open our hearts to hear you, and strengthen our hands to serve you in others for his sake; who lives and reigns with you and the Holy Spirit, now and for ever. Amen. (Collect for Mary and Martha from the Book of Common Prayer)*

7

TRUST

Relational Priorities

Guiding Principle

Trust: **Your personal rule of life is formed and reflected in your daily, weekly, monthly, quarterly and annual relational priorities.**

What are the greatest intangible gifts you've received from your family and friends? Be as specific as possible.

What are the most important gifts you can offer to those you are in relationship with (family, friends, church, work, community, etc.)?

> *Friendship is like a step to raise us to the love and knowledge of God. What happiness, what security, what joy to have someone to whom you dare to speak on terms of equality, . . . one to whom you need have no fear to confess your failings; one to whom you can unblushingly make known what progress you have made in the spiritual life!*
> —AELRED OF RIEVAULX

When you consider your primary relationships today, which offer most to your personal, spiritual development? In what ways are you contributing specifically to the spiritual well-being of others?

Biblical Reflection

**Where you go I will go, and where you stay I will stay.
Your people will be my people and your God my God. (Ruth 1:16)**

Unswerving loyalty and selfless devotion are the overarching themes of the book of Ruth, a masterpiece of literary art and theological insight. Ruth trusted in God and developed trust and trustworthiness in all of her primary relationships.

Ruth the Moabite reflects the love of God clearly and effectively. Through her benevolence she blesses her mother-in-law, Naomi, and is blessed in return with the gift of redemption. For Ruth, relational health and integrity garner life's greatest gifts of pure love, peace and joy.

Ruth is an absolutely delightful book. Mention its name and Bible readers smile, warmly praise its beauty and quietly tell what it means to them personally. The book is, after all, profoundly human—a story with down-to-earth features we can easily identify with. Immediately, readers see themselves in the story. They empathize readily with poor Naomi, battered by life's tragic blows—famine, exile, grief, loneliness—and recall their own bitter bruises. They quickly admire charming Ruth, her commitment, courage and cleverness. Admiration easily yields to emulation: readers know how much this tragic world would be better off were there more Ruths. They warm willingly to Boaz, that gracious tower of gentle manliness and generosity, whose uprightness challenges them to reflect on their own way of life. In sum, they are ordinary people who portray an extraordinary alternative to the way life is lived, the life of *hesed* ("compassionate loyalty").

The book of Ruth is a Hebrew short story told with consummate skill. Among historical narratives in Scripture it is unexcelled in its compactness, vividness, warmth, beauty and dramatic effectiveness—an exquisitely wrought jewel of Hebrew narrative art. It can be read as a drama in four acts with a prologue and epilogue. The prologue sets the scene: Naomi, her husband and two sons went to Moab, where her sons married Moabite women. Naomi's husband and sons died, and in distress she decides to leave Moab and return to her hometown of Bethlehem in Judea (Ruth 1:1-7).

In the first act, Naomi tells her Moabite daughters-in-law, Orpah and Ruth, to stay in Moab and return to their mother's home. Orpah agreed, but Ruth refused to leave Naomi and accompanies her to Bethlehem (Ruth 1:8-22). In the second act we see Ruth gathering and gleaning barley in the fields of Naomi's relative Boaz, who shows special concern for Ruth (Ruth 2). This is an obvious act of divine intervention for both Ruth and Naomi. Ruth is astounded by the favor that is shown to her as a foreigner. The comfort and kindness extended to her from Boaz is a gift from the hand of God for her love and faithfulness to Naomi.

The third act takes place at the threshing floor where, at Naomi's instigation, Ruth hides until Boaz falls asleep and then quietly lies down by his feet. When Boaz awakes, Ruth expresses her desire to marry him according to the custom of the kinsman-redeemer. But Boaz tells her that another man has a prior claim (Ruth 3). Finally, at the city gate, the other relative renounces his claim, and Boaz marries Ruth (Ruth 4:1-12). The epilogue relates Naomi's joy at this turn of events and then lists some of Ruth's descendants, including David (Ruth 4:13-18).

The book of Ruth reveals a community doing what was right in God's eyes. It's a story of God's grace in the midst of difficult circumstances. Even in times of crisis and deepest despair, there are those who follow God and through whom God works. "No matter how discouraging or antagonistic the world may seem, there are always people who follow God. He will use anyone who is open to him to achieve his purposes."

Despite our fascination with the characters of Ruth, Naomi and Boaz, God is the primary actor in the drama. Even though human beings are free moral agents, God's unseen hand directs events to accomplish his purpose. God transforms Naomi's sorrow into joy and rewards Ruth's commitment to Israel's God and community with an enduring place of honor in its heritage.

In Boaz, we see a foreshadowing of the redemptive work of Jesus Christ. "Ruth's inability to do anything to alter her estate typifies absolute human helplessness (Rom. 5:6); and Boaz's willingness to pay the complete price (4:9) foreshadows Christ's full payment for our salvation (1 Corinthians 6:20; Galatians 3:13; 1 Pet. 1:18, 19)." Loyalty, love, kindness, the value of persons and the need to understand one another stand paramount in this text. The book of Ruth tells us that no matter how bad things may be, goodness exists when we are willing to make the effort.

Ruth teaches us many lessons of loving loyalty and courageous devotion to the primary relationships of our lives. She embodies a selflessness marked by humility, gentleness and perseverance. We can all learn from Ruth in our daily attempts to foster health and vitality in our relationships.

The following list of traits that create and encompass healthy, trusting relationships are discernable from the book of Ruth. Pay close attention to how these characteristics apply to your own relationships.

- *Faithful presence.* Ruth's commitment to Naomi is a reflection of love that abides through thick and thin. When we're willing to stay for the long haul, despite the challenges, the shared experiences of life will strengthen us. Ruth's hospitality of heart wouldn't let Naomi be alone in her distress; together they embraced whatever God had for their future and were blessed as a result.

- *Honesty and transparency.* Her willingness to be fully transparent with Ruth was the key to unlocking Naomi's heart

of disappointment and heartache. As
the story unfolds, this becomes the glue
that holds them together while God's
will unfolds for Ruth and Boaz (and ultimately the extended faith community
that surrounded them). God can handle
our transparency. When we have relationships of trust, honesty and openness follow and solidify that trust.

- *Mutual submission.* Ruth was willing to
submit to Naomi's greater need for care
and empathy, even though she refused
Naomi's request to leave her side and
return to Ruth's own people. Submission to God first and foremost is the
basis of willingly submitting to the
needs of another. Openhandedness
and accountability to each other led
these two women forward. With no
need to control the outcome or each
other, God provided for them beyond
what they originally hoped.

- *Confession and forgiveness.* God's provision of a kinsman-redeemer in Boaz
is a preamble to God's gracious provision of Christ, sent to forgive, restore
and renew. In their tears Ruth and
Naomi cried out to God for comfort
and protection. And though they were
not out of God's will and in need of
confession of sin, they indeed confessed their need for redemption. Relationships that willingly voice "I'm
sorry," "I was wrong," "Please forgive
me" and "I love you" are richly blessed
by God. Only from a posture of humble repentance will reconciliation
meaningfully occur.

- *Joy: Laughter and tears.* With true joy,
despite the circumstances of their
lives, Ruth and Naomi pursue God's
perfect will. His provision of Boaz is
the apex of this love story and is symbolic of the essence of our joy in the
Lord. Out of tears of distress there are
plentiful tears of joy: "Praise be to the
LORD, who this day has not left you
without a kinsman-redeemer" (Ruth
4:14). Ultimately, Boaz and Ruth had a
son, Obed, the grandfather of King David, of the genealogy of Christ.

- *Listening and empathy.* God heard the
heart cries of Naomi and Ruth. Ruth
listened intently and empathically to
Naomi. Boaz heard from the Lord and
served Ruth boldly and lovingly. An
earnest pursuit of sympathy, empathy
and grace runs throughout this story.
Relationships that pursue a listening
posture are the most robust and life-
transforming.

- *Attitude of gratitude.* The central theme
of the story moves from emptiness to
fullness. An empty Naomi becomes
full again. An empty Ruth gleans and
gains at the threshing floor of God's
goodness, kindness and mercy. Boaz
discovers a creative way to serve the
larger cause and is richly blessed himself. With hearts of thanksgiving and
expectancy each person is filled with
God's loving will and ways. This perspective is significant for relational vitality and wholeness.

Ruth is a wonderful example of how
God delights in the quality of our earth-

ly relationships. Indeed, the entire book is filled with examples of how God blesses and multiplies the faithfulness of those who live in his grace-filled way. Ruth leaves us analyzing and reflecting on the well-ordered path toward relationship health. How is the Lord inviting you to consider this part of the journey for yourself?

1. Read Ruth 1. Naomi's famine included famine in the land and famine of her heart. The loss of her husband and two sons left her in a state of understandable bitterness and distress. What were her reasons for wanting to send her two daughters-in-law back to their Moabite families? When she arrived in Bethlehem, her focus was on emptiness and misfortune. What are the values of such authenticity?

2. Read Ruth 2–3. Ruth's commitment to Naomi and her courage toward Boaz resulted in gleaning and blessing. What are the evidences of God's faithful provisions to Ruth and all of her key relationships?

3. Read Ruth 4. Boaz's kindness and generosity toward the two widows is a foreshadowing of Christ's sacrificial role as our Redeemer. In what ways did Boaz serve as redeemer for both Naomi and Ruth?

Historical Insight

While delighting in the Lord, William Wilberforce's passion became that of God's, namely, breaking the bonds of slavery in England and the world, and in the overall reformation of society. What is remarkable about Wilberforce was his ability to attract others to share his passion. Together they accomplished many remarkable feats toward the reformation of society and the proliferation of philanthropy. Chief among his partners in changing British society were his friends in the Clapham Sect.

Wilberforce was born on August 24, 1759, to a rich merchant. A year after his father died, when William was ten, he was sent away to live with his childless aunt and uncle, William and Hannah Wilberforce, and to attend school. His aunt and uncle were evangelical Christians and close friends of George Whitefield, the famous pastor of the Great Awakening. Thus, he was exposed to lively, evangelical Christianity at a young age.

Reflecting on his childhood, Wilberforce fondly remembered hearing John Newton, the former slave-ship captain turned pastor and hymn writer, preach in London. Wilberforce was significantly affected by the preaching of Newton. William's mother became worried that her son might be "turning Methodist," so she "rescued" her son and sent him off to the boarding school Pembroke. Here, Wilberforce met William Pitt, who would eventually become the British prime minister and a powerful ally in the fight against the slave trade.

In the fall of 1776, at the young age of seventeen, Wilberforce matriculated in St. John's College of Cambridge. While in college, one of William's uncles died, leaving him a small fortune, thus ensuring he would never have to work a day in his life. Wilberforce dreamed of life as a politician. This dream fortified his friendship with William Pitt. In 1780, Wilberforce campaigned for a seat in the House of Commons to represent his hometown of Hull. Wilberforce's natural charisma and speaking ability, coupled with the £8,000 he spent on the election, secured his spot as a Member of Parliament. This election was the beginning of over half a century spent in elected office.

During his first four years as a Member of Parliament William earned a reputation among the elite of society as "a songster and wit who was professionally careless and inaccurate in method." But in 1784 Wilberforce experienced a momentous change. In a surprising turn of events he was converted to Christianity, the moment he calls "the Great Change." After this he was convicted of his frivolous and prodigal lifestyle. He understood that he had wasted his time and abilities thus far in life. One of the first effects of his new faith was contempt for his wealth, luxurious lifestyle and idleness. He developed a passion for helping the poor. Wilberforce associated his political career with his sinful lifestyle and thought that his faith and career in politics may be incompatible. He was ashamed and tormented by the idea that he may not be able to remain a politician.

Agonizing over the years he had wasted only on himself, Wilberforce wrote, "I was filled with sorrow. I am sure that no human creature could suffer more than I did for some months." Knowing Wilberforce's anguish and that he was considering stepping away from a public career, Pitt advised him to remain in politics. Though hesitant because of his reputation Wilberforce sought the advice of John Newton, who also advised him to remain in politics. One biographer suggests that Newton's advice likely mirrored a note he wrote to William two years later: "It is hoped and believed that the Lord has raised you up for the good of His church and for the good of the nation."

Once Wilberforce became a Christian and found his delight and purpose in God, his outlook on life changed. The purpose for his life was transformed. His October 28, 1787, diary entry reports: "God almighty has set before me two great objects, the suppression of the Slave Trade and the Reformation of Manners [i.e., morals]." Wilberforce devoted himself to these for the rest of his life.

The abolition of slavery and reformation of morals, however, was no small task, and Wilberforce faced severe opposition and criticism. It took forty-five years of hard work before the emancipation bill was passed in the House of Commons in 1833. In 1807 Wilberforce enjoyed his first victory, passing a bill securing the abolition of the slave trade. However, it took another twenty-six years, in 1833, before a bill was passed ensuring that abolition was actually enforced. In the beautiful providence of God, Wilberforce died on July 29, 1833, three days after abolition was passed. In addition to the abolition of slavery, during his political career Wilberforce and his allies were also responsible for founding more than 220 national religious, moral, educational and philanthropic institutions and societies to alleviate child abuse, poverty, illiteracy and other social ills.

Wilberforce leaned heavily on a group of influential friends known as the Clapham Sect. Stephen Tomkins describes the Sect as "a network of friends and families in England, with William Wilberforce as its centre of gravity, who were powerfully bound together by their shared moral and spiritual values, by their religious mission and social activism, by their love for each other, and by marriage." This group was also known as "the Saints." They included a rector, writer, governor, politician, scholar, philanthropists and musicians.

Regarding this group one historian writes,

> We are thinking of a company of men of a hundred and fifty years ago who were not only good but, by any reasonable measurement, great. They applied themselves to the social and religious problems of their time not only with zeal but with wisdom. They undertook the overthrow of gigantic evils and succeeded in their undertaking. They initiated movements which, so far from having spent themselves, are vigorous and powerful today.

Never a formal organization, the Clapham Sect was a company of friends who lived near each other in a quiet village near London. They shared the same religious outlook and worked together in close cooperation for the good of the world.

They were a remarkable Christian community, bound together not only in friendship but as coworkers in the kingdom of God. They exercised their philanthropy on a generous scale. They were keenly interested in the new missionary movement. In addition to ending the slave trade, the Clapham Sect was also credited with the foundation of the Bible

Society, whose purpose was to enable more people to have a Bible, and many other valiant endeavors for the good of the society at large.

Many members of the Clapham Sect were influential, and several were wealthy. They did not retreat from society but rather applied their Christian faith and their influential position in society to reform it. One way was through philanthropy. One year Wilberforce gave away £3,000 more than he earned. Though he didn't always give more than he earned, he routinely gave away a quarter of his income. Through a generous, well-ordered heart, and in the context of healthy, trusting relationships, William Wilberforce and the Clapham Sect have left an indelible mark on the world. They are to be applauded for their affect on subsequent generations of Christians in the marketplace of business, politics and social change.

Personal Rule of Life

1. Review the "roles" section previously completed. List here the relationships that occupy the majority of your time. What are the greatest joys and blessings of each of these relationships?

2. Now review the same list of relationships, and list the greatest needs of either the relationship itself or the individual or group involved. Note carefully, empathically and prayerfully the situation(s) that have contributed to these needs.

In what ways is God inviting you to recalibrate your earthly relationships? In questions 1-3 you will be encouraged to prayerfully consider the state of your primary relational connections. In order for your strengths and weaknesses to be identified side by side, it's important to be candid in your reflections. As you address these issues alone, consider ways to reveal your discoveries to those most directly affected. This section of your rule of life will impact all other areas yet to be revealed.

3. Attend to your own emotional state for a few moments. What feelings or emotions are you dealing with that need some attention? Are you dealing with any sense of desolation or discouragement in reference to these relationships? Or are there any emotional concerns rising up from deep within that you'd like to seek help to better understand? (Be sure not to avoid what rises to the surface; seek professional counsel as needed.)

4. Who are the people that mean the most to you? Do you feel called to deepen those relationships so they continue to be a source of ongoing encouragement and enrichment? If so, how?

After answering questions 4-6, take time to begin writing the personal rule of life statements below.

5. Do you feel called to come alongside some of your key relationships in order that healing, hope, forgiveness or restoration can occur? Explain.

6. Take some time to consider your relational and emotional development priorities for the upcoming season of your life. Put these into meaningful phrases or sentences that will enhance trust within the key relationships noted. Don't try to be comprehensive here. Instead, prayerfully ask the Lord to lead you to the relationships or emotions of greatest priority.

	TRUST: YOUR RELATIONAL PRIORITIES
Daily/regularly	
Weekly	
Monthly	
Quarterly/seasonally	
Annually	

Spiritual Community

1. What was most striking to you about the relationships Ruth had with both her mother-in-law Naomi and her husband Boaz? How was this story of redemption an encouragement to you?

2. As you read about the amazing life and service embodied in William Wilberforce, what strikes you as his greatest contributions? How do you think his relationships with his peers enhanced his work?

3. As you consider the health and strength of your primary relationships, what are your observations about how churches or organizations are (or are not) aiding you in developing healthy relationships?

4. As you've been reflecting on the health of your primary relationships, what positive or negative emotions were brought to the surface? Why is it important for us to attend to our emotional state, particularly as it affects our primary relationships?

5. How can we come alongside one another as spiritual friends, praying, encouraging and exhorting each other to focus on the health and vitality of our primary relationships?

Lord, the gift of relationship is one that you have offered to your people since creation. When I consider the work of your hands, the primary gift you have bestowed on your people is a relationship with yourself. But you also invite us to interact with one another in families, churches, organizations, communities, businesses and schools. Help me to look candidly in my heart and lead me to be a positive influence in all spheres of my daily life. I ask this for the sake of your kingdom, the building up of your church, the encouragement of your people and the honor of your name, Father, Son and Holy Spirit. Amen.

8

TEMPLE

Physical Priorities

❖

Guiding Principle

Temple: **Your personal rule of life is formed and reflected in your daily, weekly, monthly, quarterly and annual physical priorities (the care and training of your body, mind and heart).**

What descriptive words come to mind when you look in the mirror and review with integrity the current state of your physical health and well-being? Do so with candid honesty, but avoid self-deprecating terms as much as possible; consider more affirming and realistic ones instead.

> *Do you not know that your body is a temple of the Holy Spirit, who is in you, whom you have received from God? You are not your own; you were bought at a price. Therefore honor God with your body.*
> —1 CORINTHIANS 6:19-20

What descriptive words would you like to be able to say about your desired or preferred state of physical, emotional and intellectual health and well-being in the future? What roadblocks stand in the way of making this a reality?

Write a short prayer that conveys both your current and preferred state of physical, emotional and intellectual health and well-being. Offer your full self into the loving embrace of God, who holds you securely in the palm of his loving hand and generously extends his grace to you, particularly in this area of your personal life.

Biblical Reflection

For you created my inmost being;
    you knit me together in my mother's womb.
I praise you because I am fearfully and wonderfully made;
    your works are wonderful,
    I know that full well.
My frame was not hidden from you
    when I was made in the secret place.
When I was woven together in the depths of the earth,
    your eyes saw my unformed body. (Psalm 139:13-16)

The U.S. Department of Health and Human Services recently released its objectives for "Developing Healthy People 2020," and the list is pretty impressive. Some of the goals in the "Physical Activity and Fitness" category include increasing the proportion of adults and adolescents that meet current federal physical activity guidelines for aerobic activity and for muscle strength training; modifying childhood and adolescent television viewing and computer use; and increasing the proportion of trips made by walking or bicycling.

The program also includes objectives in thirty-eight other areas, such as access to health services, adolescent health, cancer, diabetes, family planning, mental health, nutrition and weight, oral health, sexually transmitted diseases, substance abuse, and tobacco. Each of these arenas of physical health and well-being are designed to offset our society's growing obesity (which is hovering near 30 percent) and, on the other end, our obsession with weight loss. The latter is evidenced in the increasing epidemic of eating disorders, such as bulimia and anorexia, particularly among younger women.

The evidence is everywhere: diet fads, fitness clubs, detox cleansers, lap-band surgery, just to name a few. Our society has gone overboard addressing the need to care for our bodies. The media has convinced us of the impossible—you can look like a bodybuilder or a supermodel. The truth is that the majority of us fall miserably short of this unreachable goal.

Also, within the Christian community there are a growing number of resources available to those who struggle with addictive behaviors of all kinds. *Addiction* is defined as a state of powerlessness and inability to manage one's life because of a physical or emotional dependence on an outside agent. Often these addictions fester from within, because of our inability to measure up to society's expectations. In addition to alcohol and drug abuse (illegal and prescription), many individuals face addictions to pornography, inappropriate sexual relationships, gambling and other harmful behaviors. The need is growing, and so is the wherewithal to help those who suffer.

Our world is incredibly stressful. Change is constant. Mobility is the new norm. Expectations are heightened everywhere. Time pressures continue to increase. Work life is uncertain. Competition and schedule overload is demanding more and more of our lives. Relationships are fraught with dysfunction and affected by illness, divorce, distress and aging. We have an overabundance of food, of finances and of power, which leads to gluttony, to selfishness and to manipulation and pride. We are a culture out of control.

Whatever happened to the wisdom of "all things in moderation," "take things one step at a time," "if it's too good to be true, then it probably is," and "if you want to see genuine change, then you need to genuinely change"? Our equilibrium has been lost and has been replaced by the quickest, fastest and least painful way to reach a goal.

What's the antidote to a lifestyle in which our bodies are no longer the temple of the Holy Spirit? Jesus invites us to

an internally motivated pursuit of the kind of balance he had. He "grew in wisdom and stature, and in favor with God and man" (Luke 2:52). We gain favor with God and others by balancing our physical stature with our pursuit of wisdom.

Supplementing Jesus' balanced approach, the apostle Paul says,

> I have learned to be content whatever the circumstances. I know what it is to be in need, and I know what it is to have plenty. I have learned the secret of being content in any and every situation, whether well fed or hungry, whether living in plenty or in want. I can do everything through him who gives me strength. (Philippians 4:11-13)

Yes, contentment with a sincere attitude of gratitude helps us overcome the pressure to make our physical bodies more important than God intends. Contentment opens the door for the Holy Spirit to reside fully in our heart, mind and life.

As a pastor friend of mine once quipped, "Our body is the temple of God. Therefore, be careful where it goes; be careful what it consumes; be careful what it does; be careful what it ponders; be careful how it reacts." Or as another pastor reminds his readers,

> "I am fearfully and wonderfully made." This is something I struggle with. I look on my skinny frame and distinct lack of biceps and feel that I have missed out in the hand-

someness stakes. It was only as I did some reading about artificial intelligence and computer programming that I began to realize that my arm is a marvel that no robot arm can match, my eyes are wonders no camera can ever come close to. My ability to walk over all kinds of terrain, ride bicycles, climb cliffs and swim through water is not matched by any vehicle that man has made despite billions of dollars of research. And with my nervous system I got a free multi-media supercomputer with self-programming capacity! At birth! For free! Unearned! My first degree was in chemistry and the ability of the liver to synthesize complex macromolecules out of last night's dinner is mind-boggling. No chemist could go anywhere near it.

God loves your physical body and it is very precious to him. He is our Creator. Jesus demonstrated his love for our bodies when he healed so many needy people. And God dwells in our bodies, calling them his temple. Our bodies are sacred sites where God delights to reside today. And he has promised a future for our bodies; after this life he offers us resurrected bodies that will last forever.

As you continue the process of developing your personal rule of life, consider the following suggestions for the care of your body. Treat it with holy obedience and submit it to God's intended purposes as an act of worship. Your body is the temple of the Holy Spirit, a place where God resides and desires to reign supreme.

Rest your body. Whenever necessary, reduce the stress your body is absorbing in this fast-paced life. Consider ways to simplify your lifestyle; follow a schedule that's more conducive to a balanced life; get the necessary sleep your body needs (averaging eight hours each night); and practice sabbath rhythms and disciplines for at least one twenty-four-hour period each week. One of the best ways to care for your heart and mind is to ensure that your body gets the rest it needs—don't underestimate the importance of physical rest.

Replenish your body. Be sure to eat balanced meals and watch unnecessary calorie and carbohydrate intake. Take vitamins and additional nutrients according to your body's needs (consult your physician); practice good self-care, dress and grooming that fits your lifestyle and honors the Lord. Keep your mind stimulated with appropriate intake—what you read and watch impacts how well you're being replenished. Focus on "whatever is true, whatever is noble, whatever is right, whatever is pure, whatever is lovely, whatever is admirable—if anything is excellent or praiseworthy—think about such things" (Philippians 4:8).

Renew your body. Schedule annual physical exams and biannual dental cleanings, and don't let physical symptoms linger before seeing a physician. Take your allotted vacation, and maximize the time away for rest and refreshment; exercise a few times each week. Address any addiction that plagues you, and seek professional and communal help to overcome and be restored. Enjoy hobbies and recreational activities that restore and enhance your creative well-being.

Release your body. Don't make an idol of your body by caring more for it than you care for your soul or your relationships. Give your appetites and temptations to the Lord so his priorities are yours. In preparation for eternity, hold your life loosely and open-handedly, and embrace the certainty of your mortality by seeing death as an entrée into heaven and the presence of God. Consider prayerfully the eternal promises of heaven—living forever in a new and perfect body.

Solomon, David's son, was anointed king of Israel before his father's death (1 Kings 1:17-39). He began his reign well but made a foolish mistake in choosing a pagan king's daughter for his wife. Despite being known for his wisdom, he confessed his weakness, ignorance and need for a discerning heart. God granted him this desire, promising that Solomon would be the wisest of men and would have great riches and honor. Solomon composed 3,000 proverbs and a 1,005 songs.

As his wealth and honor increased, so did his love for a luxurious and extravagant lifestyle, beyond the means or the resources of his people (1 Kings 10:14-29). This led to social discontent and the downfall of his kingdom. In this downward spiral, Solomon plunged into sensuality and apostasy. Even though known for his wisdom, he did not have self-control. He taught well but failed to practice his own precepts. He is widely considered the author of Proverbs, Ecclesiastes and Song of Songs, books with practical teaching on real-life issues of "right living."

What do we learn from Solomon? In the care of our physical bodies, we need not only wisdom but also the fruit of God's Spirit, self-control (cf. Galatians 5:22-23; 1 Corinthians 10:23–11:1). Only by and through the power of God's Spirit will we be able to adequately treat our bodies in God-honoring ways. May his Spirit guide you as you bring order to this part of life.

1. *Meaningless and folly.* Read Ecclesiastes 1–2. Notice how the author defines so much of the physical world as "meaningless." Identify for yourself which aspects of your physical life lead you into madness and folly, and the ways the care of your body leads you into wisdom and sensibility. How easy is it for you to teeter between the two?

2. *Wisdom and awe.* Read Ecclesiastes 3, 5 and 7. Notice the ways that wisdom leads us to the reverence and awe of God. When we live under the umbrella of God's Word

and wisdom, what is the result? How does this apply to the care of your body as a temple of the Holy Spirit?

3. *Obedience and faithfulness.* Read Ecclesiastes 10–12. Notice how wisdom is better than strength, better than the best weapons of war.

> The heart of the wise inclines to the right.
> Words from the mouth of the wise are gracious.
> As you do not know the path of the wind,
>   or how the body is formed in a mother's womb,
> so you cannot fully understand the work of God.

How do obedience and faithfulness to God lead us into deeper joy than any physical pleasure can offer?

Historical Insight

One of our heroes in the faith, St. Augustine, struggled with the care of his physical body, particularly as it related to the area of lust. This is such a huge issue in our day as well. Augustine was chosen for this chapter so we can learn from his wrestling and find freedom to live within the bodies God has given to us. Those who pursue a holistic personal rule of life desire this as part of honoring and pleasing the Lord as our Creator, Redeemer and Sustainer.

Augustine was born in Thagaste (in modern-day Algeria) in A.D. 354. His education began in Thagaste and he was eventually sent to Carthage to complete his education. He studied rhetoric and became a powerful and persuasive orator.

While studying in Carthage in 371 he wrote of "the din of scandalous love-affairs raged cauldron like around me."

> My soul's health was consequently poor. It was covered with sores and flung itself out of doors, longing to sooth its misery by rubbing against sensible things; yet these were soulless, and so could not be truly loved. Loving and being loved were sweet to me, the more so if I could also enjoy a lover's body; so I polluted the streams of friendship with my filthy desires and clouded its purity with hellish lusts.

Augustine took a concubine at age seventeen, and lived with her for fifteen years. She bore him a son, Adeodatus, which means "given by God."

Augustine struggled not only with lust but also with acting on it. Before he was converted, his carnal desires were making him extremely miserable, and he pleaded to God for the gift of chastity, praying, "Grant me chastity and self-control, but please not yet." He knew his mental and physical behavior was detrimental but it was so powerful that he would rather satisfy than snuff out his lust.

Augustine was greatly influenced by Manichaeism (one of the religious sects of his day) because it provided what seemed to him the best response to evil. However, "so much of him plainly did not belong to this oasis of purity: the tensions of his own passions, his rage, his sexuality, his corrupt body." When he became a Christian he affirmed that the body is good. Humans are both body and soul. All creation, including our physical bodies, are good, but since the Fall they have been perverted and abused by us.

Augustine moved to Milan in 384 to seek new opportunities and success. While in Milan he heard Ambrose preach and was impressed that Ambrose could defend the Old Testament against Manichaean criticisms. Augustine was seriously wrestling with the truths of Christianity and the doubts that fluttered in his mind. Eventually the levy of his soul broke with a flood of tears and emotion streaming from Augustine's eyes and heart. In 386 he converted to Christianity.

"I flung myself down somehow under a fig-tree and gave free rein to the tears that burst from my eyes like rivers, as an acceptable sacrifice to you." And he said, "O Lord, how long? How long? Will you be angry forever? Do not remember our age-old sins." "Why must I go on saying, 'Tomorrow . . . tomorrow'? Why not now? Why not put an end to my depravity this very hour?" Immediately after this outburst he heard the voice of a child from a house nearby repeatedly singing, "Pick it up and read, pick it up and read." He understood this to be a divine command and remembered the story of St. Anthony, who had a similar experience with the providential reading of Scripture. Augustine obeyed the voice of the Lord, snatched up a Bible, opened it and read the first passage his eyes landed on.

He read Romans 13:13-14: "Let us behave decently, as in the daytime, not in orgies and drunkenness, not in sexual immorality and debauchery, not in dissension and jealousy. Rather, clothe yourselves with the Lord Jesus Christ, and do not think about how to gratify the desires of the sinful nature." As soon as he finished reading these verses he was fully assured of his faith and all shades of doubt fled away. Upon his conversion Augustine left the career of rhetorician and teacher. Augustine's conversion was not marked by a turn to a prudish "morality of joyless conscientiousness" but rather from the love of a second-rate beauty to that of supreme beauty, namely God.

In 387 Augustine was baptized by Ambrose. By 391 Augustine arrived in Hippo to establish a monastery and was ordained a priest. In 395 he was made the bishop of Hippo, the vocation he faithfully fulfilled through preaching, writing and debating the heresies of his day (Manichaeanism, Donatism, Pelagianism) until he died in 430.

The following are some notable quotes from Augustine related to our physical bodies as the temple of the Holy Spirit. Each is worthy of our prayerful reflection. What of the following leaps off the page and into your heart?

> Even the natural pleasures of human life are attained through distress, not only through the unexpected calamities that befall against our will but also through deliberate and planned discomfort. There is no pleasure in eating or drinking unless the discomforts of hunger and thirst have preceded them. (*Confessions* 8.3.7)

> However far a man may fall away from the truth; he still continues to love himself, and to love his own body. The soul which flies away from the unchangeable Light, the Ruler of all things, does so that it may rule over itself and over its own body; and so it cannot but love both itself and its own body. (*On Christian Doctrine* 1.23.22)

> He is to be taught in what measure to love his body, so as to care for it wisely and within due limits. For it is equally manifest that he loves his body also, and desires to keep it safe and sound. (*On Christian Doctrine* 1.25.26)

> For to enjoy a thing is to rest with satisfaction in it for its own sake. To use, on the other hand, is to employ whatever means are at one's disposal to obtain what one desires, if it is a proper object of desire; for an unlawful use ought rather to be called an abuse. (*On Christian Doctrine* 1.4.4)

> When the impetuous power of the soul is viciously inclined, and it swaggers in mutinous, insolent pride, violent crimes are the outcome; when the appetite of the soul which thirsts for carnal pleasures is not moderated, vices are the result; so too, if the rational mind itself is vicious, errors and wrong-headed opinions corrupt our life. (*Confessions* 4.15.25)

Personal Rule of Life

1. When is the last time you've visited a doctor, dentist or dietician? What is your current routine for such visits?

2. When is the last time you were on a regular diet and/or exercise program? What is your current routine in this regard?

Since our bodies are a temple for the Holy Spirit, we need to take a close look at how well we are caring for our physical well-being. There are daily regimens to consider, as well as sporadic and regular routines that require our diligent attention. In questions 1-3 we will address these important issues. Be frank in your replies; ultimately it will affect your health and well-being. This issue matters to God and will have ripple effects on those who love you most and who are your companions on the way.

3. List the current ways you are resting, replenishing, and renewing your body, heart and mind. Which aspect needs the greatest attention right now? How will you accomplish this?

4. *Diet, exercise and rest.* What are your desired dietary, exercise and rest (both sabbath and sleep) priorities? Be specific.

Take time now to begin writing personal rule of life statements from questions 4-6.

5. *Hobbies and recreation.* What are your desired hobby and recreational priorities? Be specific.

6. *Heart and mind.* What are your desired emotional and intellectual priorities? Be specific.

TEMPLE: YOUR PHYSICAL PRIORITIES	
Daily/regularly	
Weekly	
Monthly	
Quarterly/seasonally	
Annually	

Spiritual Community

1. How does Solomon's love for a luxurious and extravagant lifestyle parallel our world today?

2. As Augustine struggled with self-control, he found that the fruit of God's Spirit challenged the lusts of this world. In what ways does his wrestling with lust speak to our age?

3. If you are willing, show the members of the group your "Temple: Your Physical Priorities" column. Why is this either an affirmation, embarrassment or inducement toward pride?

4. How did it feel to answer questions of such a personal nature in this section? What emotions (e.g., fear, anxiety, shame, freedom, joy) emerged as you considered each question? Have you noticed a correlation between your physical and spiritual health? Why is this such a challenging area for us to consider?

5. How can we pour courage (or accountability) into each other's hearts as it relates to developing habits that contribute to our physical health and the well-being of our body, heart and mind? In what ways do you want to be prayed for by your friends?

Lord, help me to care for my body in ways that honor you. The fact that my body serves as a temple for the Holy Spirit is staggering to consider. I want to feed, clothe and care for this body in ways that please you and reflect your priorities for my daily life. By your grace and for your glory, give me godly discipline to provide all that my body needs, but not all that it wants. Give me wisdom and understanding beyond what I have had to date, and guide me into a future that invigorates and energizes my body toward your loving purposes. Have your way in me, O Lord. In the name of the Father, Son and Holy Spirit. Amen.

TREASURE

Financial Priorities

Guiding Principle

Treasure: **Your personal rule of life is formed and reflected in your daily, weekly, monthly, quarterly and annual financial and material stewardship priorities.**

Jesus clearly warns his disciples to be careful about where their treasure is stored, whether in heaven or on earth. Linger prayerfully for a few moments and consider how many of your treasures are focused on heaven. What makes for a heavenly possession? What are you storing up for heavenly purposes?

> *Do not store up for yourselves treasures on earth, where moth and rust destroy, and where thieves break in and steal. But store up for yourselves treasures in heaven, where moth and rust do not destroy, and where thieves do not break in and steal. For where your treasure is, there your heart will be also.*
> —MATTHEW 6:19-21

Now reflect on your earthly possessions. Which can be destroyed by moths? Which have the propensity to rust? If stolen by thieves, which of your possessions would you miss the most?

Prayerfully release your earthly possessions into the hands of God. If placed in his hands, which do you think he would hand back to you because they are rightfully placed in your heart, and which do you think he would withhold because they possess your heart? Write a prayer of release, letting go of (detaching from) your worldly possessions and being set free from worrying about your "valuables" on earth. Pray instead that you might become attached to God and his kingdom priorities.

Biblical Reflection

No one can serve two masters. Either he will hate the one and love the other, or he will be devoted to the one and despise the other. *You cannot serve both God and Money.* **Therefore I tell you, do not worry about your life. . . .** *But seek first his kingdom and his righteousness, and all these things will be given to you as well.* **(Matthew 6:24-25, 33, emphasis added)**

There are hundreds of Bible verses on stewardship, generosity, money, possessions and their effect on the hearts and lives of God's people. Where do we begin to unpack the subject of our earthly treasures? Do an online search and you'll be blurry-eyed with the plethora of stewardship resources available to the body of Christ. The crux of the matter is that it's all about the heart.

Heartfelt stewardship and generosity was an important priority for the early church. When the Holy Spirit arrived at Pentecost and filled all the believers, they asked themselves in amazement and perplexity, "What does this mean?" (Acts 2:12). When Peter stood to address the crowd, he quoted from the prophet Joel:

I will pour out my Spirit on all
    people. . . .
I will show wonders in the heavens
    above
    and signs on the earth below. . . .

And everyone who calls
    on the name of the Lord will be
      saved. (Acts 2:17, 19, 21)

He also quoted from David in Psalm 16:

You have made known to me the
    paths of life,
    you will fill me with joy in your
      presence. (Acts 2:28)

He called all within earshot to repentance and forgiveness, to be baptized and receive for themselves the gift of the Holy Spirit. About three thousand were added to their number on that day.

They devoted themselves to the apostles' teaching and to the fellowship, to the breaking of bread and to prayer. Everyone was filled with awe, and many wonders and miraculous signs were done by the apostles. *All the believers were together and had everything in common. Selling their possessions and goods, they gave to anyone as he had need.* Every day they continued to meet together in the temple courts. They broke bread in their homes and ate together with glad and sincere hearts, praising God and enjoying the favor of all the people. And the Lord added to their number daily those who were being saved. (Acts 2:42-47, emphasis added)

This result is repeated again in Acts 4:32-35 (emphasis added):

All the believers were one in heart and mind. *No one claimed that any of his possessions was his own, but they shared everything they had.* With great power the apostles continued to testify to the resurrection of the Lord Jesus, and much grace was upon them all. There were *no needy persons among them.* For from time to time *those who owned lands or houses sold them*, brought the money from the sales and put it at the apostles' feet, and it was distributed to anyone as he had need.

What a scene of biblical obedience and community provision! Treasures stored up in the hearts and lives of the believers for heavenly purposes were freely shared in this incredible experience of faith, hope and love. Imagine if this would be the case today.

Barnabas is a great example of someone who held his treasures loosely and offered them for kingdom-building purposes. Acts 4:36-37 says, "Joseph, a Levite from Cyprus, whom the apostles called

Barnabas (which means Son of Encouragement), sold a field he owned and brought the money and put it at the apostles' feet." Contrast that account with the one that follows. In Acts 5:1-2 we read of Ananias and Sapphira, who also sold a piece of property and placed it at the apostles' feet, but with one major difference. Unlike Barnabas, they withheld some of the money.

Peter confronts both Ananias and Sapphira. He chastises them, saying that Satan had filled their hearts and as a result they lied to the Holy Spirit by keeping for themselves some of the money. After they heard Peter's rebuke they fell down at his feet and died on the spot. Great fear seized the whole church when they heard of these events.

Gripped by an ungodly heart of earthly greed, Ananias and Sapphira lost their lives. Overcome with godly gratitude and heavenly joy, Barnabas is blessed by God.

The state of Barnabas's heart is evidenced in a handful of Scriptures that provide more detail about his life. We not only know of his generosity but learn of his warm-heartedness, demonstrated in the fact that "when he arrived [in Antioch] and saw the evidence of the grace of God, he was glad and encouraged them all to remain true to the Lord with all their hearts" (Acts 11:23). We are also told of his wealth of spiritual insight: "He was a good man, full of the Holy Spirit and faith, and a great number of people were brought to the Lord" (Acts 11:24).

In addition to his generosity, warm-heartedness and spiritual insight, we know he made at least five great contributions to the early church. All of the following reflect a life attuned to God's stewardship priorities. Barnabas's impact on the early church was a reflection of his internal convictions coming from a heart aflame with the love of Christ.

Advocacy (Acts 9:23-31). Led by the Holy Spirit, Barnabas introduced Saul (Paul) to the apostles and urged them to see the authenticity and sincerity of his conversion. Although the early church leaders were skeptical, Barnabas recognized Paul's genuine heart for God and his great potential. As a result, Paul was accepted by the early church leaders and commissioned to serve in Jesus' name.

Integrity (Acts 11:19-30). Barnabas was a man of integrity who had spiritual eyes to see it in others. He represented the apostles in Antioch when, for the first time, Gentiles had been evangelized in significant numbers. He saw this as a genuine movement of God and by his encouragement, fanned the flame of church growth. He was the kind of person who brought people together; he continuously reminded and urged them to keep their hearts close to the Lord.

Servanthood (Acts 13:1-2, 46-49). Barnabas was set apart with Paul for the work of the Spirit. As commissioned ones, they were released to serve in ministry and set apart for God's purposes. As a result of their bold proclamation, the word spread throughout the region. In this passage we see the names reversed (v. 46)—Barnabas was now serving Paul.

Passion (Acts 14:12-14, 21-22). Barnabas and Paul were passionate about the work they were called to. They ran away from all human adulation and instead served to the glory of God. They strengthened the disciples and encouraged them to remain true, even when suffering hardships, knowing that it is through hardships that we enter the kingdom of God.

Faithfulness (Acts 15:1-29). Barnabas was appointed with Paul to defend the gospel before the Jerusalem Council. He answered tough theological questions about God's gracious work of salvation among the Gentiles. Barnabas revealed his heart as a true shepherd of the flock of God, even to the point of confronting and disputing false doctrine in the church.

As the "son of encouragement" Barnabas was always spurring people to action, motivating them to do good and building up their faith. He was an advocate for genuine faith and church life. He lived a life of integrity and hopefulness. He passionately served Christ and made long-term commitments to faithfully stand with others in service for the gospel. What a heart—what a life—what a great steward of all that was entrusted to his care. Barnabas serves as an inspiration for all who want to be faithful stewards of their God-given treasures.

1. Read one of the five passages (listed above) about Barnabas's contributions to the early church (advocacy, integrity, servanthood, passion and faithfulness). What do you discover about the heart of this man from this text?

2. In what ways does the life of Barnabas—the encourager—reflect the heart and priorities of Jesus: "For where your treasure is, there your heart will be also" (Matthew 6:21)?

3. Prayerfully read the following passages on generosity of heart: 1 Chronicles 29:10-13; Luke 21:1-4; 2 Corinthians 8:1-7. What do they have in common, and how do they apply to your heart today?

Historical Insight

Five minutes after I die, what will I wish I would have given away while I still had the chance?
—Randy Alcorn

Stewarding our life of abundance includes how we handle our earthly treasures, and it grows outward into every aspect of our lives. Our treasure and our heart are intertwined in more ways than are obvious.

Two centuries ago George Mueller spent over sixty years in Bristol, England, preaching, leading the Scripture Knowledge Institute and caring for orphans. He is widely known for refusing to receive a salary during the last sixty-eight years of his ministry. He also refused to ask people for money. Instead, he constantly prayed, asking God to meet his and thousands of orphans' needs. And God was faithful. A man after God's own heart, he properly managed the resources entrusted to his care and lived a life of authentic generosity.

Mueller cared deeply about the Scriptures and the faith of God's children. Though he predominantly worked with orphans, Mueller viewed all Christians as God's children. He claimed that everything he did, especially how he handled money, was to increase the faith of Christians. Mueller's entire life was devoted to encouraging the faith of God's children. He did this primarily through the financial resources provided by God through the generosity of God's people. Mueller was much more concerned with faith than with money; however, he knew that the love of money often stifles faith. Thus, the way he dealt with money was a key factor in his devotion to Christ and in his ministry.

Born in Kroppenstaedt, Prussia (modern-day Germany), on September 27, 1805, George's father preferred him over his younger brother—which proved very injurious to both boys. While they were still children, their father gave the boys a lot of money, "not in order that we might spend it, but, as he said, to accustom us to possess money without spending it." His father sent George to a cathedral classical school in hopes that his son might become a clergyman, not to serve God but that he might have a comfortable living.

George spent his time in school studying, reading novels and indulging in riotous living. At the age of fourteen his mother died. He wasn't aware of her illness, and the night she was dying he was up until 2 a.m. playing cards. The next morning, a Sunday, he and some friends went to a tavern and roamed the streets half drunk. His teenage years were spent in a cycle of sinful behavior, setting resolutions to turn from his vices and then failing to keep them.

He entered Halle University and became a student of divinity. Here Mueller had a dramatic conversion:

And now at a time when I was as careless about Him as ever, He sent His Spirit into my heart. I had no Bible, and had not read in it for years. I went to church but seldom. I had never heard the Gospel preached up to the beginning of November, 1825. I had never met with a person who told me that he meant, by the help of God, to live according to the Holy Scriptures. In short, I had not the least idea that there were any persons really different from myself, except in degree.

After his conversion Mueller had a strong desire to become a missionary, but his father was displeased, saying that he had invested so much money in George's education in hopes that he might comfortably live out his last days with him in his son's parsonage. During his years at Halle University George resolved not to take any more money from his father, which he was able to keep. Rather than continue under his father's support, the Lord provided money for Mueller as a translator for American scholars studying in Halle.

In early 1826 Mueller lived in the Orphan House because poor divinity students could stay there free. In 1829 he moved from Berlin to London, hoping to become a missionary with the London Missionary Society. But George eventually realized he did not see eye-to-eye with the Society, so he severed his connection with them.

As a result, he began to preach wherever he could. He spent some time with a small congregation (eighteen people) in

Teignmouth, and they eventually invited him to be their pastor. His initial salary was £55 (about $200 at that time), and this increased as the church grew. On October 17, 1830, Mueller married Mary Groves. At the end of October 1830 Mueller gave up his church salary and instead put a collection box in the chapel so that whoever desired to contribute to his support could put an offering inside. About this Mueller wrote,

> At the same time it appeared to me right, that henceforth I should ask no man, not even my beloved brethren and sisters, to help me, as I had done a few times according to their own request, as my expenses, on account of travelling much in the Lord's service, were too great to be met by my usual income. For unconsciously I had thus again been led, in some measure to trust in an arm of flesh; going to man instead of going to the Lord at once. To come to this conclusion before God, required more grace than to give up my salary.

Around the same time he and his wife also decided to take literally the Lord's commandment to "Sell your possessions and give to the poor" (Luke 12:33). On November 18, 1830, they had only eight shillings, which is roughly $2.

In 1835 Mueller began working toward establishing his first orphanage.

> I had constantly cases brought before me, which proved that one of the special things which the children of God needed in our day, was, to have their faith strengthened. Sometimes I found children of God tried in mind by the prospect of old age, when they might be unable to work any longer, and therefore harassed by the fear of having to go into the poor-house. If in such a case I pointed out to them, how their Heavenly Father has always helped those who put their trust in Him, though they might not always say that times have changed; yet it was evident enough, that God was not looked upon by them as the LIVING God. My spirit was ofttimes bowed down by this, and I longed to set something before the children of God, whereby they might see, that He does not forsake, even in our day, those who rely on Him.

On April 11, 1836, the First Wilson Street Orphan-House was opened. During the beginning of orphan work, Mueller's funds were low and he relied on God to provide. On October 19, 1836, Mueller opened the Second Wilson Street Orphan-House.

> To-day we obtained, without any trouble, through the kind hand of God, very suitable premises for the Infant Orphan-House. If we had laid out many hundreds in building a house, we could scarcely have built one more suitable for the purpose. How evident is the hand of God in all these matters! How im-

portant to leave our concerns, great and small, with Him; for He arranges all things well! If *our* work be *His* work, we shall prosper in it.

On October 21, 1837, the Third Wilson Street Orphan-House was opened. All in all he built five orphan houses and cared for over ten thousand orphans during his lifetime.

Mueller devoted himself to the oversight and leadership of the Scriptural Knowledge Institute, the orphanages, and to preaching and teaching God's Word. In fact, from 1834 to 1875 he devoted himself to preaching tours. At the ripe age of seventy Mueller did not retire but rather decided to pursue his lifelong dream of being a missionary. So from 1875 to 1892

he toured the world preaching, and God provided for all of his financial needs.

He preached in over forty countries over the span of over twenty-five years, often preaching every single day. Regarding his preaching tours Mueller writes, "In the course of the last seventeen years, having travelled about 200,000 miles altogether, by land and by sea, in the Lord's service, my dear wife and I have abundant reason to praise God for having sustained us in health and vigour of mind and body up to the present time." His was an amazing life indeed—a model for those interested in laying down the treasure of this world, trusting God for daily needs and watching the hand of God gently and miraculously at work.

Personal Rule of Life

1. What words or phrases best describe the ways you manage your material and financial resources?

2. What material or financial resources or concerns have a grip on your soul, are of disproportionate importance to you and as a result need to be held more loosely?

3. If given the opportunity, what would you want to change about your current abili-

Do you understand how much God cares about your finances and how well you are stewarding all that you have for his glory? As you read the accounts of faithful believers in the biblical and historical text, what is your response? In this section we find ourselves guided humbly into an area of heartfelt concern. How you are handling your treasure is a good indication of the current state of your heart. As you answer questions 1-3, reflect with honesty; don't hold back your thoughts. Be sure not to approach this with any manner of pretense or angst. There's freedom in telling the truth, particularly in this regard.

ties to steward your material and financial resources? It might be helpful to look at the past six months' financial activities—bank account, investment portfolio, personal/family budget and credit card statements—and pray over these while formulating your answer to this question.

4. As you reflect prayerfully on your material and financial life, what do you sense the Lord is inviting you to adopt as new or renewed practices? For example, not spending more than __ dollars per month on coffee or on clothing, or fasting from the cinema for a certain number of months and giving the money saved to charity.

As you answer questions 4-6, take time to begin writing the personal rule of life statements below.

5. With whom are you discussing this priority? What would be most helpful from others to help you forge ahead in this area of life?

6. In what ways do you desire more simplicity in your material and financial stewardship priorities?

	TREASURE: YOUR FINANCIAL PRIORITIES
Daily/regularly	
Weekly	
Monthly	

Quarterly/seasonally	
Annually	

Spiritual Community

1. In what ways does Barnabas's example encourage your heart and stimulate you to reconsider your personal pursuit of godly stewardship and generosity?

2. How did reading about George Mueller bring joy to your heart and in what ways does his godly example of generosity and financial freedom encourage you to act similarly?

3. Why is it so difficult or challenging to discuss financial matters when we are so free to discuss most other areas of life with one another? If you are willing, show the members of the group your "Treasure: Your Financial Priorities" column.

4. What are the guiding principles that matter most in stewarding your personal material and financial resources?

5. What are the primary practices that guide you in this area of your life and service to others? Invite others in your group to pray for you in this regard, recognizing to-

gether that "where our treasures are, there are our hearts also." This verse is critical for understanding and unifying our spiritual and financial priorities.

Lord Jesus, regarding my money and resources: do they own my heart, or am I stewarding them well? Your words are ringing in my heart—where my treasure is, there is my heart also. Where is my heart today, Lord? I submit to your loving embrace and your honest evaluation. Where the things of this world have a grip on my heart, help me to release them. Where I value my possessions more than I honor you, the Lord of all, forgive me and grant me your compassion. Where I long for things that have been created more than you, the Creator of all things, grant me your peace. I want my heart to treasure that which you treasure, Lord. May it be so today, for you and you alone are the center of my heart and the lover of my soul. In Jesus' name. Amen.

10

TALENT

Missional Priorities

❖

Guiding Principle

Talent: **Your personal rule of life is formed and reflected in your daily, weekly, monthly, quarterly and annual missional priorities.**

Over the past week or month, when, where and with whom did you sense you were being Christ toward others? How did your personal gladness of heart mesh with the particular need of the moment?

In what ways did someone else become for you a Christlike portrayal of missional focus and encouraged your heart? How did that person's fulfillment of their personal mission move you toward a fuller release of your own mission?

> *The calling of all of us, is the calling to be Christ's. To be Christ's in whatever way we are able to be. To be Christ's with whatever gladness we have and in whatever place, among whatever brothers we are called to. That is the vocation, the destiny to which we were all of us called even before the foundations of the world.*
> —FREDERICK BUECHNER, *SECRETS IN THE DARK*

As you consider broadly the mission God has for his people in this world, which aspect is most compelling to you and why?

Biblical Reflection

**Noah found favor in the eyes of the Lord . . . a righteous man,
blameless among the people of his time, and he
walked with God. (Genesis 6:8-9)**

What are you summoned to do with your life? The Bible is filled with examples of how God lovingly and specifically called and set apart his chosen ones to fulfill God-sized vocational callings.

Abraham was chosen by God to become the father of a new spiritual people (Genesis 12:1-4; Hebrews 11:8-10). Joseph, the favored son of Jacob, lived a God-honoring life but suffered great trials at the hands of his jealous brothers and Egyptian leaders. His forgiveness of his brothers (Genesis 45:3-15) and his gift of returning good for evil (Genesis 50:15-21) put him in a unique place in biblical history. God installed Joshua into his role as Moses' successor with provisions for success (Joshua 1:1-5). During his career of conquest, Joshua experienced multiple supernatural events that served to protect him and the people of Israel under his care (Joshua 3:14-17; 5:13-15; 6:2-5, 12-21). As a result, he conquered thirty-one kings, and most of Canaan was subdued under his leadership.

There are so many others who had specific callings: Daniel, the statesman and prophet; Gideon, the mighty warrior; Elijah, the prophet of fire; Elisha, the prophet who receives a double portion of the Spirit; Nehemiah, the team and wall builder; Jonah, the stubbornly resistant follower; Paul, the apostle of grace and faith; Stephen, the martyr.

Though our list could go on, the one to focus on here is Noah. Noah, first spoken of in the Scriptures at the ripe age of five hundred, was the grandson of Methuselah, the longest living man (Genesis 5:27), and the great-grandson of Enoch, a man of notable piety who escaped death by being taken away by God (Genesis 5:24; Hebrews 11:5). Noah stems from a fascinating lineage indeed.

Noah lived in a desperately corrupt age. Humans had become so depraved that the Lord determined to destroy the entire race (Genesis 6:1-7). In the midst of such moral darkness, Noah's life shined with the radiance of righteousness (Genesis 6:8-9). God revealed to Noah that a great flood would destroy all humanity. God's absolute disdain for human evil made him regret creating them.

Thus, Noah was given a very strange and, from a human perspective, impossible task. Noah was called to construct an immense boat for preserving his own family and representatives of the animal kingdom. The dimensions of the ark are a bit uncertain, but it was huge. The length was approximately 450 feet, the width 75 feet and the height 45 feet (with a commonly assumed length of 18 inches per cubit). This feat, which seems impossible or at least highly improbable even by today's standards, became a vocational call of epic proportions for Noah.

As Noah began to build the ark, he exhorted the people who observed and undoubtedly mocked him (2 Peter 2:5). Their scoffing made Noah a laughingstock, but it did not hinder his work. He maintained his faith and toiled on, year after year. It took so long that they must have thought he had gone mad. His work over many years stands unsurpassed and unequaled among all other biblical characters. Few others are like Noah in his persistent faith and unswerving obedience to the clarion call of God.

Noah built the ark

because a voice had told him to. . . . Only a fool would heed such a voice at all when every other voice for miles around could tell him, and probably did, that our proper business is to keep busy: to work, to play, to make love, to watch out for our own interests as everybody else does, and to leave the whole shadowy business of God to those who have a taste for shadows. So Noah building his ark becomes the bearded joke draped in a sheet who walks down Broadway with his sandwich-board inscribed REPENT; and Noah's face becomes the great white moon face of the clown looking up with anguish at the ones who act out their dance of death on the high wire. A penny for your thoughts, old Noah, as you pound together your zany craft while the world goes about its business as usual and there is not a cloud in the sky.

Contrary to the skeptics, God sent rain and the water covered the whole earth. After the rains had stopped for several months, Noah sent out a dove from the ark to see if the waters had indeed receded from the earth. When the dove returned with a freshly plucked olive leaf, Noah's heart leaped with joy and hope. The little sprig of hope is held up against the world's intolerance to faith, hope standing in stark contrast to ridicule. The power of hope is evident from the moment Noah first received his instructions to build the ark to the final days of the flood waters.

On the heels of the flood, God's wonderful promise of the rainbow signifies his perpetual commitment to all future generations. Noah built an altar (the first recorded altar in the Bible) and offered a sacrifice (Genesis 8:20); he planted a vineyard, which led him to sin (Genesis 9:21); and died a fulfilled man of God (Genesis 9:28-29).

Noah, a righteous man, blameless among the people of his time, found favor in the eyes of the Lord (Genesis 6:8) and walked with God, doing everything just as God commanded. Noah stands as an example of tireless commitment to his calling. God knew the heart of Noah and gave him an enormous mission to fulfill amid a crooked and perverse generation. The ark is a symbol of vocational service for all future generations of believers. What a legacy: a man after God's own heart, who heard the command to a specific mission and heeded it against all odds.

1. As you ponder the significance of Genesis 6, what strikes you most about the heart, favor and call of God? How does this stand in contrast to the disobedience of humanity?

2. Read Genesis 7–8, the flood account. Do you see the theme of hope throughout the preparations for the flood, the experience in the ark and the postflood experiences? Explain.

3. Now read Genesis 9. What are the specifics of God's covenant with Noah? (Be sure to include the rainbow and Noah's drunkenness.) What theme ties this chapter together, and how is this an encouragement to you?

Historical Insight

When one lives obediently in the center of a call, one feels God's pleasure; one knows joy. Let us be frank: men and women have obeyed God's call and become martyrs. Others have undertaken unspeakably difficult and discouraging tasks and barely survived. Some have lived obscure lives in far off corners of the world and have finished the course never feeling that they accomplished anything of measurable value. There have been others, of course, whose lives have sparkled with results— who in their preaching, their writing, their organization-building, and their ability to envision and empower people have left their mark on church history. What did they all have in common? They felt God's pleasure; they had joy.

Fanny Crosby, the remarkably gifted poet and hymn writer, had a strong sense of mission. She was born on March 24, 1820, to John and Mercy Crosby, in Putnam County, New York.

At six weeks she was blinded by medical malpractice. Her blindness never held her back from fulfilling the life mission ordained for her by the Lord. She was an excellent student and a gifted poet.

While teaching at the New York Institute for the Blind she had a student, Alexander Van Alstyne, who later returned to teach at the school. They fell in love, and on March 5, 1858, they were married. For the first five years or so after they were married Fanny did very little writing and devoted her energies to being a wife and mother.

In December 1863 her pastor requested that she write a poem for a church service. She happily obliged. Then during the first days of 1864 the same pastor connected Fanny to William B. Bradbury, a famous hymn writer. She promised Bradbury she would provide lyrics to a hymn within a week. Just three days later she submitted the verses to her first hymn, "Our Bright Home Above." Bradbury published the hymn later that year. Referring to this incident, Fanny commented, "My real work as a hymn-writer began from that hour. *I had found my mission*, and was the happiest creature in the land. Mr. Bradbury lightened many of my darkest days and scattered sunshine over my hours of care" (emphasis added).

Shortly after, Mr. Bradbury requested a patriotic hymn (the Civil War had been going on for three years). Fanny wrote the words to complement the rhythm and measure of the already-written tune. After hearing the song Bradbury said, "How in the world did you manage to write that hymn? Nobody ever supposed that you, or any other mortal, could adapt words to that melody. . . . Fanny, I am surprised beyond measure. . . . Let me say that as long as I have a publishing house, you will always have work."

Fanny studied great poets, loved learning the Scriptures and possessed an incredible memory. She "memorized eight complete books of the Bible and on at least two occasions she composed hymns in groups of forty and retained them all in her memory before writing any of them on paper."

Mr. Bradbury developed tuberculosis in the fall of 1867. Knowing his end was near he told Fanny of his condition. Greatly upset by the news she said, "Oh must I lose a friendship that I have enjoyed so much?" To this Mr. Bradbury replied, "No, take up my lifework where I lay it down; and you will not indeed lose a friendship, though I am going away from you, but rather strengthen it by striving to carry out my own ideals."

Referencing her vision and specific mission in life Fanny observed,

> I have sought each day to be one of God's unselfish souls. From the time when I received the first check for my poems I made up my mind to open my hand wide to those who needed assistance. During these ninety years I have never served for mere pay. I have always wanted to do a full day's work regardless of what the financial results might be. He who only works for pay gets nothing more. Gold is good in its place, my dear friends, but when it becomes our master, it places a crown of thorns upon the brow that crushes the strongest to the earth.

In addition to writing hymns Fanny was in high demand for speaking engagements at civic, patriotic and religious meetings. Her popularity continued to escalate and remains to this present day as many of her hymns still occupy prominence in worship settings worldwide. In her lifetime she wrote over eight thousand hymns, spoke before Congress and met several presidents.

In 1903 Fanny wrote:

The poor doctor, who spoiled my eyes, soon disappeared from the neighborhood and we never heard any more about him. He is probably dead, before this time; but if I could ever meet him, I would tell him that unwittingly he did me the greatest favor in the world. If I could meet him now, I would say, "Thank you, thank you"—over and over again—for making me blind, if it was through your agency that it came about! Why would I not have that doctor's mistake—if a mistake it was—remedied? Well, there are many reasons: and I will tell you some of them. One is that I know, although it may have been a blunder on the physician's part, it was no mistake of God's. I verily believe it was His intention that I should live my days in physical darkness, so as to be better prepared to sing his praises and incite others so to do. I could not have written thousands of hymns—many of which, if you will pardon me for repeating it, are sung all over the world—if I had been hindered by the distractions of seeing all the interesting and beautiful objects that would have been presented to my notice.

Some of Fanny's greatest hymn titles include "Safe in the Arms of Jesus" (Fanny's favorite), "Redeemed," "Saved by Grace," "Blessed Assurance" and "To God Be the Glory," all worthy of our prayerful reflection today. One of my favorites is "Pass Me Not, O Gentle Savior." Fanny wrote this hymn after speaking at a prayer service in a prison, and she heard one of the prisoners shout, "Savior, do not pass me by." Let the words of this hymn sink deeply into your soul and offer them up as your own prayer of deliverance and freedom.

Pass me not, O gentle Savior,
Hear my humble cry;
While on others Thou art calling,
Do not pass me by.

Refrain
Savior, Savior,
Hear my humble cry;
While on others Thou art calling,
Do not pass me by.

Let me at Thy throne of mercy
Find a sweet relief,
Kneeling there in deep contrition;
Help my unbelief.

Refrain

Trusting only in Thy merit,
Would I seek Thy face;
Heal my wounded, broken spirit,
Save me by Thy grace.

Refrain

Thou the Spring of all my comfort,
More than life to me,

Whom have I on earth beside
    Thee?
Whom in Heav'n but Thee?

Personal Rule of Life

1. Where and with whom are you *currently* investing yourself in service to others? This can include the marketplace, community, church and family, domestically or abroad.

2. Where and with whom do you *desire in the future* to invest yourself in service to others? Again, this includes the marketplace, community, church and family, domestically or abroad.

God's invitation to fulfill his call becomes clearer as you get closer to his heart. Listening intently to his Word in prayer combined with community discernment is essential. When God calls he makes the mission clear. His voice and his will is most specifically evident in a life of faithful love and obedience. In questions 1-3, count on the reality of God's mission—and all the accompanying details—to become apparent as you attend to his voice of invitation. There is no greater joy than living in the center of his divine will. Pursue that with your whole heart and trust others to help guide you toward the well-ordered way, your personal rule of life.

3. In what ways do you need further training, assistance or partnership with others in order for your personal mission priorities to be fulfilled?

4. Return to the mission statement you crafted previously and analyze whether that statement is in alignment with your current investment of yourself in service to others. How should this statement be revised to keep these priorities in focus?

Take time now to begin writing the personal rule of life statements in questions 4-6.

5. As you prayerfully review your current and desired places of missional service, which areas are most life-giving? Should any be eliminated because they have come to an end or the situation has changed and they are inappropriate investments of your gifts and calling?

6. Use the following chart to record your priorities for stewarding your missional priorities.

	TALENT: YOUR MISSIONAL PRIORITIES
Daily/regularly	
Weekly	
Monthly	
Quarterly/seasonally	
Annually	

Spiritual Community

1. Noah "found favor in the eyes of the LORD." What does the term *favor* mean today, and who does it apply to in our modern context?

2. Fanny Crosby's ability to overcome enormous odds helped her focus on what mattered the most. In what ways can we maintain focus on fulfilling our mission, and how is her example an inspiration to you today?

3. Our missional priorities can change over time, and as we get older they become more pronounced. How are you sensing stability or change in your personal mission during this particular season of life?

4. Discuss together how you are sensing the Lord's invitation to a deeper fulfillment of your personal missional focus. If you are willing, show the members of the group your "Talent: Your Missional Priorities" column.

5. Share with each other a specific prayer request for discernment, clarity and focus in one area of your personal missional priorities.

Lord Jesus, to serve another in your name both delights and concerns my heart. When I am living in the power of your Spirit, I am giving myself away to others with joy. I simply offer my life as a living sacrifice, wholly and completely out of love for you and for others. Help me when I'm unaware of or not abiding in you, but am serving out of my own strength, for my own applause or for other selfish motives. Pierce my conscience with a greater attentiveness to my need to be needed, and give me a sense of your empowerment and call. I long to be a reflection of Christ in this world, representing you well and pointing others to you for the sake of your glory, the building up of your kingdom and the honor of your name. Father, Son and Holy Spirit. I delight in you today. Help me by your grace, love and mercy to be your servant toward all who cross my path. Amen.

Weaving Together Your Personal Rule of Life

Your personal rule of life is a holistic description of the Spirit-empowered rhythms and relationships that create, redeem, sustain and transform the life God invites you to humbly fulfill for Christ's glory.

For the past five chapters we have been forming a personal rule of life around the five major priorities of life: spiritual, relational, physical, material and missional. These capture the essence of how we utilize our time, trust, temple, treasure and talent all for the glory of God. As we reflected on the biblical and historical texts, you began to identify how your life is to be lived out in similar fashion. Each step of the way included questions for further reflection and processing with others. Now it's time to summarize what you've jotted down in the previous five chapters and capture your thoughts on one large chart. Either use these two pages for that purpose or create your own version. Be sure to consider all of these areas of your personal life but don't feel compelled to fill in every blank area or it may seem too restrictive or overwhelming. This exercise is designed to be life-giving, so approach it with prayerful openness and receptivity to the leading of God's Holy Spirit.

YOUR . . .	TIME	TRUST	TEMPLE	TREASURE	TALENT
Daily/ regularly					
Weekly					

YOUR . . .	TIME	TRUST	TEMPLE	TREASURE	TALENT
Monthly					
Quarterly/ seasonally					
Annually					

PART THREE

Fulfilling Your Personal Rule of Life

In John 17 we discover, through a fabulous prayer of Jesus, the essence of God's heart for the unity of his disciples worldwide and throughout all generations. . . .

Pause and reflect for a moment on the thought, if we love someone we are always dreaming of their future and planning for their greatness. Does that concept resonate with your spirit? Are you that kind of lover of others within the body of Christ—in your family, in your circle of friends, among colleagues, and with fellow believers in your local church and the extended Christian community? Disciples of Jesus Christ become lovers of others within the faith community as a direct reflection of how Jesus has loved us as his disciples. It may feel rather circular in thought and design, and in fact it is. The prayer in John 17 ascribed to Jesus himself is very much that way—he prayed for himself; he prayed for his disciples; he prayed that the love he had from the Father would remain in him and be given away to his disciples who in turn would share it with one another so the world would know about the love of the Father through his Son and fulfilled in the unity of disciples everywhere and for all generations! Dizzy yet? It may feel as though it keeps going round and round, but in actuality it's drilling the truth deeper and deeper into the inner recesses of the disciples' hearts.

STEPHEN A. MACCHIA, *BECOMING A HEALTHY DISCIPLE*

COMMITMENT TO
THE BODY OF CHRIST

❖

Guiding Principle

As a member of the body of Christ, your personal rule of life is formed, released and fulfilled within the context of a covenantal faith community of worship, love and service—in fulfillment of the Great Commandment (loving God with heart, soul, mind and strength), the Second Great Commandment (loving neighbor as you love yourself), and the Great Commission (loving others and making disciples in Jesus' name).

What is the name of the local congregation where you currently worship and participate in the life of a relational and missional community? What words or phrases best describe the spiritual health of this faith community? If you are currently not involved in a specific local church, what are the reasons that keep you from making such a commitment today?

Overall, what are the greatest reasons or benefits of maintaining a solid and consistent commitment to a faith community? In what ways would you like to see that com-

One of our chief blind spots has been to overlook the central importance of the church. We tend to proclaim individual salvation without moving on to the saved community. Our message is more good news of a new life than of a new society. . . . This vision of a renewed human community has stirred me deeply. At the same time, the realities of the lovelessness and sin in so many churches are enough to make one weep, for they dishonor Christ. Yet increasing numbers of church members are seeking the church's radical renewal. For the sake of the glory of God and the evangelization of the world, nothing is more important than the church becoming God's new society.
—JOHN R. W. STOTT, *EPHESIANS*

mitment deepened by yourself and others in the future? If you are currently not involved in a specific local church, what would encourage you to do so in the future?

Summarize the way in which you pray for unity in the body of Christ and specifically for your local church family. Or if you aren't praying for the wider body of Christ or your congregation today, what do you think would be most appropriate to request of the Lord on the church's behalf? In a paragraph or two write a prayer that conveys your sentiments for God's worldwide church and for your local church.

Biblical Reflection

I have given them the glory that you gave me, that they may be one as we are one: I in them and you in me. May they be brought to complete unity to let the world know that you sent me and have loved them even as you have loved me. (John 17:22-23)

We now shift into how our rule of life is lived in the wider body of Christ. Within our specific faith community context, our relationships are found in the local church, in other ministry settings and among trusted spiritual friends. Those who know us best love us and wish us well as we follow the path of life God invites us to fulfill. Therefore, oneness, unity and covenantal love are to be our shared priority.

Oneness in the body of Christ is of paramount importance for Jesus. In John 17 we find one of Jesus' most extensive and profound prayers. Here, Jesus' teachings regarding the unity of the Godhead conclude, this time in the form of a prayer.

He prays for unity among his disciples and expresses his deep love for the ongoing work of God among future generations. This prayer highlights the world's separation from God, his unconditional love for the people of this world and the disciples' mission to reach the world with the gospel—all for the glory of God.

As with much of Jesus' farewell discourse, this material is complex and can be outlined in several ways. Jesus begins with a petition for the glorification of the Father and the Son (John 17:1-5), after which he prays for the disciples gathered around him, first describing their situation (vv. 6-11) and then praying for their protection and sanctification by God (vv.

11-19). Jesus then prays that all who will become believers may share in the divine oneness (vv. 20-24). He concludes with a summary of his past and future work (vv. 25-26).

In Jesus' final recorded prayer we are encouraged to consider the primacy of the body of Christ within our own prayers. The Son's coming to earth brought the presence of God's love into this world, and when Jesus enters the hearts of believers he offers a love that transforms. The focus of Jesus' prayer is intimacy between Jesus and the Father, Jesus and his disciples, the disciples among themselves, and the ministry of the disciples toward the unbelieving world. It is precisely because Jesus abides in them that they in turn receive the love of the Father.

The twofold abiding, Christ in us and we in him, is what creates the oneness we experience with one another. All that Jesus did prior to this prayer and all that he has done subsequently is in response to God's righteous will. And Jesus' will for oneness among his children reflects his own perfect life of light and love. Oneness is the place where we begin—both with God and with one another as the people of God. As we all live out our respective rule of life, we combine our lives to fulfill God's rule together as members of his eternal family.

In the early church, unity was experienced primarily because of the Holy Spirit's activity among the believing community. Beginning with Pentecost, the unity within the church was possible only through the transformative work of God's Spirit. When the Spirit was not in their midst (having been shunned or ignored), unity was dismantled by the work of the flesh. The church couldn't be reunited through self-effort, but by receiving it as a gift from the Lord and inviting God's Spirit back into their midst.

> For he himself is our peace. . . . His purpose was to create in himself one new man out of the two. . . . He came and preached peace. . . . For through him we both have access to the Father by one Spirit. . . .
>
> In him the whole building is joined together and rises to become a holy temple in the Lord. And in him you too are being built together to become a dwelling in which God lives by his Spirit. (Ephesians 2:14-15, 17 18, 21-22)

Christ himself is our peace—he came and preached peace. Therefore together we are to become a single dwelling place in which God lives by his Spirit. Paul's words to the church in Ephesus sums it up for us today. By his Spirit we are united in Christ, and our focus is on the peaceful ways we are to live among one another, always in a manner worthy of our calling. "Be completely humble and gentle, be patient, bearing with one another in love. Make every effort to keep the unity of the Spirit through the bond of peace" (Ephesians 4:2-3).

Therefore, as we live out our personal rule of life in the context of the body of Christ, we do so most effectively in the unity of God's Spirit. In 1 Corinthians 12 Paul writes to the church about this same matter. When utilizing the gifts of the Spirit, do so in a unified way. He uses the analogy of the body, which is one unit made of many parts, all parts needing the other. They are created and arranged by God himself—just as he wanted them to be. Seventeen times in 1 Corinthians 12 Paul repeats the word *body* to describe how we are to function in a united fashion. We must, he says, always be concerned equally for each other, so that when one part suffers, every part suffers, and when one part is honored, every part rejoices.

Unity in the body—Jesus prayed for it, the early church experienced it, and Paul commended it among the believing community. We are desperate for it today, and when we cry out to the Spirit to grant us our heart's desire, he delivers with surprising unity in the body. The greatest example and most excellent way is love, the glue that holds together common unity.

How then do we experience the oneness and unity that Jesus prays for and the Spirit sustains? Through love. When love reigns supreme, the body of Christ expresses love as patience, kindness, truthfulness, protection, trust, hope and perseverance—not with envy, boastfulness, pride, rudeness, selfishness, anger, keeping grudges or delighting in evil (1 Corinthians 13:4-8). Love extravagantly expressed never fails; it's held together by the covenant faithfulness of the triune God, which Jesus invites his followers to join.

So it is with those who are seeking to fulfill a rule of life within the context of the body of Christ. Love guides us forward and leads us into the path of life that honors and pleases God. Love is the benchmark, the essential ingredient, the foremost priority and the foundation on which all else is built. Without love, there is no community. And without love, there is no oneness or unity within that community.

The author of the book of Hebrews puts it this way:

> Therefore, brothers, since we have confidence to enter the Most Holy Place by the blood of Jesus, by a new and living way opened for us through the curtain, that is, his body, and since we have a great priest over the house of God, *let us draw near to God* with a sincere heart in full assurance of faith, having our hearts sprinkled to cleanse us from a guilty conscience and having our bodies washed with pure water. *Let us hold unswervingly to the hope we profess*, for he who promised is faithful. And let us consider how we may spur one another on toward love and good deeds. *Let us not give up meeting together*, as some are in the habit of doing, but *let us encourage one another*—and all the more as you see the Day approaching. (Hebrews 10:19-25, emphasis added)

The only way such covenantal love is to be upheld in the body of Christ is if all persevere. We must draw near to God, hold unswervingly to the hope we profess, continue to meet together and encourage one another.

It's all about *love*—as Jesus resides in us, we are invited to abide in *him*: loving because he first loved us, loving others and ourselves as he loves, sharing his love with all who cross our path. And it's all about persevering—individually and collectively—in the life God has invited us to fulfill for his glory! Covenantal love is the hallmark of a healthy church today. It's the fuel for persevering in fulfillment of God's purposes.

1. Read Jesus' great high-priestly prayer in John 17. Ponder prayerfully verse 23. What do you notice here about the Trinity? What about the priority of unity for the body of Christ? How does unity impact the presentation of the gospel in this world? What's the invitation here for you today?

2. Prayerfully consider Ephesians 4:1-6. What is God's desire for you and your community within the body of Christ? If you were to make this your daily prayer, what do you think would emerge in your heart toward others in your faith community?

3. Read Hebrews 10:19-25. Several places begin with "let us" in this text. What are God's priorities in these places, and in what ways is God asking his children to reflect these priorities within their respective faith community?

Historical Insight

It makes a difference *how one thinks about the church*. Thinking of it as an organization *dictates one way of going* . . . thinking of it as an organism demands a totally different *modus operandi*. When the organizational aspect is primary—*size of membership, building and budget are decisive* . . . and measurable. When its organic nature is primary—*quality of life, attitudes, relationships are decisive* . . . and they do not yield easily to measurement.

When considering the priority of the

church and our commitment to remaining steadfast in our membership within the body of Christ, one leader stands above the rest, John Calvin. Although Calvin did not initiate the Reformation (that was Martin Luther), he played a major role in defining it theologically and embodying it in the local church. He faithfully lived out his personal rule of life, and generations of Protestants have benefited from his enormous contributions. We all can appreciate him no matter our theological persuasion. This is particularly true in relation to his strong theological arguments for the necessity of the church.

John Calvin was "a man of order and peace born into a world of conflict. [H]e, the man who understood the need for unity better than any other in his century, was, before he died, to see not merely three major 'churches' in Europe, . . . but religious dissensions breaking out into the first of the savage civil wars." Calvin was born on July 10, 1509, to Gérard and Jeanne Calvin in the Picardy region of France. His father, the notary for the cathedral as well as registrar to the ecclesiastical court, intended John for the priesthood at an early age. At around age 12, John became a clerk for the bishop and received the tonsure, which was a symbolic portrayal of his dedication to the church.

John was educated in Paris and excelled in school, particularly in the classics. He earned his masters by the age of sixteen or seventeen. (He most likely needed special permission for this be-cause masters students of the time typically needed to be at least twenty-one.) Though set for a career in theology or in the church, when John was about twenty years old his father took him from Paris and sent him to the University of Orleans to study law. In the spring of 1531 Calvin's father died and this liberated Calvin so he could return to study what he loved, the classics.

Sometime between 1528 and 1533 Calvin was fully converted and on board with the Reformation. In 1533 Calvin is believed to have assisted his friend Nicholas Cop, the rector of the University of Paris, in composing a sermon that lambasted the Paris theologians. This infuriated the Paris establishment, who sought to have Cop arrested for heresy. Cop fled and Calvin left with him, ending up in Basel, Switzerland. This was Calvin's first active role as a reformer.

In 1536, while in Basel, Calvin wrote the first edition of his most famous work, the *Institutes of the Christian Religion*. In 1559, while in Geneva, Calvin completed his final edition of the *Institutes*, which was expanded to such a degree that he considered it a new work. If Calvin could have had it his way, he would have lived a peaceful, academic life. In a letter to a friend he wrote, "The summit of my wishes was the enjoyment of literary ease, with something of a free and honourable station." Later he writes, "I have learned from experience that we cannot see very far before us. When I promised myself an easy, tranquil life, what I least expected was at hand."

What Calvin was least expecting was an invitation to work to reform the church in Geneva. Calvin, when he had heard of the state of things in this turbulent city, refused. He was, he said, a scholar, not a man of affairs. Besides, he had no aptitude for such a work; he was shy and nervous. The response he got was, "You are simply following your own wishes; and I declare in the Name of almighty God that if you refuse to take part in the Lord's work in this Church, God will curse the quiet life you want for your studies."

Calvin felt called to Geneva and devoted to the ministry of striving "to realize the idea of the Church that he believed to find in the New Testament and the early Church." It wasn't that Calvin necessarily *desired* to be in the center of conflict or to work in the church in Geneva, rather, he went to Geneva out of obedience to what he felt God had called him to. Calvin placed a heavy emphasis on unity within the church. In his commentary on Ephesians 4:11-14, Calvin says,

> Our true completeness and perfection consist in our being united in the one body of Christ. What is more excellent than to produce the true and complete perfection of the church? The church is the common mother of all the godly, which bears, nourishes, and brings up children to God, kings and peasants alike; and this is done by the ministry.

Calvin was the head pastor of the Church of Geneva and was dedicated to "proclaiming the Word of God" and "in-structing believers in wholesome doctrine." As a pastor Calvin was busy with the typical duties of officiating weddings, baptizing infants, and visiting the sick and troubled, but his primary task as pastor was in preaching the gospel. To edify the church God gave Calvin the gift of teaching and preaching. Calvin's method for preaching was to preach through the Bible book-by-book.

> On Sundays he took always the New Testament, except for a few Psalms on Sunday afternoons. During the week, apart from occasional high festivals, it was always the Old Testament. He began at the beginning of a book and expounded it passage by passage, clause by clause, day after day, until he came to the end. Then he started on another book.

Calvin continuously stressed the importance of the church working together in a fashion consistent with the Scriptures and the experience of the early church.

> Luther and Calvin were no firebrand revolutionaries, but responsible men who saw around them a Church which made a mockery of the New Testament picture of the Church. They dared not, having God as their Judge, draw back from the task to which they were impelled of calling the Church to reform herself in accordance with the Scriptures.

The political and religious landscape of Switzerland made for a great deal of diversity. Each of the towns in Switzerland were politically independent and so were free to choose their own religion. Many towns were Roman Catholic while many were Reformed. However, even among the Reformed cities there was still a great diversity: some were influenced more by Zwingli, others by Luther, others by Bucer and some by Calvin. Calvin worked tirelessly to unite the Reformed towns and their respective churches.

Calvin's hard work and patience paid off; in 1549 the Reformed Churches in Switzerland were united in their subscription to the Consensus of Zurich, which Calvin and his Zwinglian contemporary Heinrich Bullinger wrote together.

Even Calvin's death sparked unity among the body of Christ.

> When he died, all Geneva desired to see his body, as if he were a medieval saint or one of those relics that he had so sardonically mocked. He had seen to it that there should be no posthumous canonization and left orders that he should be buried in an unmarked grave. Thus his death and burial were of one piece with his life; as a good witness, he would not be regarded, but bent all his energies in life and death to making Jesus Christ alone great, and making that greatness visible.

To know Calvin best one must read his remarkable theological treatises, most notably his *Institutes of the Christian Religion.* Calvin wrote extensively on the subject of the church; the following are a few examples for prayerful consideration and reflection.

> The church is called "catholic," or "universal," because there could not be two or three churches unless Christ be torn asunder [cf. 1 Corinthians 1:13]—which cannot happen!
>
> "For what God has joined together, it is not lawful to put asunder" [Mark 10:9], so that, for those to whom he is Father the church may also be Mother. And this was so not only under the law but also after Christ's coming, as Paul testifies when he teaches that we are the children of the new and heavenly Jerusalem [Galatians 4:26].
>
> The church is referred to as the communion of saints and this means that "each of us should keep in brotherly agreement with all God's children, should yield to the church the authority it deserves, in short, should act as one of the flock.

Further, the title "community of saints"

> very well expresses what the church is. It is as if one said that the saints are gathered into the society of Christ on the principle that whatever benefits God confers upon them, they should in turn share with one another. This does not, however, rule out diversity of graces, inasmuch as we know the gifts of the Spirit are variously distributed.
>
> If truly convinced that God is the

common Father of all and Christ the common Head, being united in brotherly love, they cannot but share their benefits with one another.

What is the church according to Calvin?

Wherever we see the Word of God purely preached and heard, and the sacraments administered according to Christ's institution, there, it is not to be doubted, a church of God exists [cf. Ephesians 2:20].

Calvin believes that

there is nothing that Satan plots more than to remove and do away with one or both of these. Sometimes he tries by heaping contempt upon them to drag us away from the church in open rebellion. By his

craft the pure preaching of the Word has in some ages disappeared.

Calvin does not differentiate between a person who has been saved and a member of the church. The forgiveness of sins admits one into the church. Likewise, only the members of the church enjoy the forgiveness of sins. There is no individual Christianity—Christianity is only "the communion of saints."

To understand the priority of the church we must be somewhat familiar with at least one of the giant figures of the Reformation. John Calvin's writings remain paramount today for pastors and church leaders alike. The fulfillment of Calvin's rule of life has had tremendous positive implications for all generations of Christians since the Reformation.

Personal Rule of Life

1. How are you currently contributing to the unity of the body of Christ within your community or region? Do you have attitudes or actions that need to change; if so, what and how will that occur?

2. How are you currently contributing to the health of your local church? What attitudes or actions can you display that will lead others to be positive, life-giving agents of spiritual health and vitality in your congregation?

It's one thing to give lip service to the priority of unity and oneness in the body of Christ, and another thing altogether to contribute to it. In this section you will be given opportunity to add your own personal reflections on the priority of the local church. In addition, you will be invited to prayerfully consider how you can contribute to the ongoing edification of the church. Prayerfully ponder questions 1-3.

3. How is the Lord inviting you to a deeper commitment to serving others within the context of your local church or other places of ministry?

4. In what contexts of life and service are you in a covenantal relationship (where there is a written covenant that defines your life together as a community)? How widely is this covenant understood and embraced? Create a one-sentence statement about your personal commitment to the body of Christ.

    Take time now to begin writing the personal rule of life statements in questions 4-6.

5. If you aren't in a covenantal relationship (spiritual community, local church or other group), where and with whom do you feel most drawn to that kind of relational commitment? Craft a brief statement about how your personal rule of life will be lived out in the body of Christ.

6. Does your local church (or faith community) have a written covenant or community rule of life? In what way(s) can you aid in writing and/or reviewing it for prayerful consideration?

Spiritual Community

1. The Bible is filled with "one anothers" that define our life in community (e.g., love one another, serve one another, bear one another's burdens, pray for one another, forgive one another). How has a "one another" been expressed in your group recently?

2. John Calvin crafted statements that define and celebrate the unity in the body of Christ. What aspect of his writings noted in this chapter was most impressive to you and why?

3. Most of us deny that we resist submission to the larger good of the church. How have you seen this resistance within yourself, and how can you encourage one another to become more of a positive influence in the larger context of the body of Christ, even when you don't necessarily agree?

4. Why do you think it's so hard to write, fulfill, maintain and sustain a community covenant or shared rule of life?

5. If you were starting to create a covenant from scratch, what would you consider important to include? (Articulate the context, size, purpose and design of the group you are discussing if different from your present group.)

Lord, my local church is not perfect, most likely because I'm there along with others who don't mean to make a mess of your church but we do. Forgive me for taking advantage of the faith community for my own purposes and not upholding the priority of love for your Bride. I know that you, Father, have a deep and profound love for the church, and I pray that your heart for the church would increasingly shape my heart as well. May I be renewed by your Spirit to reflect the "one anothers" that are so clear in your Word. Even this coming week, may I see loving, serving, praying with and bearing with one another come alive in my own experience. Give me eyes to see, ears to hear and a heart that resonates with the needs of the church. For your sake, Father, Son and Spirit. Amen.

CONTEXT OF A
SPIRITUAL COMMUNITY

❖

Guiding Principle

Within the context of a spiritual community, your personal rule of life is released and fulfilled through the blessing, encouragement and support of a small group of spiritual friends who understand and affirm your deepest desires as well as provide the intimacy of transparent, loving and prayerful accountability.

We are created for relationships. We are not destined to live in isolation. We need each other in order to grow and become all that God intends. What are the reasons for the independence and loneliness often experienced today?

Fear can often keep us from pursuing intimacy in human relationships. What are those fears, and which do you relate to most specifically in your own experience with family, friendships, workplace, community and so on?

Discernment, indeed the whole Christian experience, is like a dance with God. God in his love and holiness invites us into a dialogue, a conversation, a relationship that includes not only submission but also the engagement of our will and our freedom with God.

We never discern in isolation; we discern in community. Every significant choice we make reflects the fact that we are profoundly interconnected with the lives of others. Our decisions inevitably affect others but we are also affected by the choices that others make. It is only appropriate that we are accountable to others in our choices; others need to be able to challenge us and confirm whether what we believe to be God's will is truly of God. We need the wisdom and counsel of others.

—GORDON SMITH, *LISTENING TO GOD IN TIMES OF CHOICE*

Prayerfully consider ways to open yourself up to others in your sphere of influence. What would you like to offer to the Lord in prayer as you embrace your rule of life within the context of spiritual friends accompanying you on your life journey?

Biblical Reflection

Love must be sincere. Hate what is evil;
cling to what is good. Be devoted to one another in brotherly love.
Honor one another above yourselves. Never be lacking in zeal,
but keep your spiritual fervor, serving the Lord. Be joyful in hope,
patient in affliction, faithful in prayer. (Romans 12:9-12)

Throughout the Bible we see evidence of spiritual community, particularly among a handful of friends who stuck together no matter what. Some of the more remarkable stories include Moses' brother, Aaron, and his friend Hur, who were sent to Moses' side to hold his arms in times of worship and prayer. David had Jonathan to encourage and protect him, and Nathan to bring him to his knees in confession. Naomi had Ruth, her devoted daughter-in-law who stuck by her at a critical time of grief, loss and rebuilding of life. Noah had his wife and sons, who endured with him the ridicule of his peers and helped him build the ark. Elijah had Elisha, Samuel had Eli, and Mary had Elizabeth. Jesus had his disciples, but particularly close to him were Peter, James and John.

One remarkable story of spiritual friendship occurs in the Gospels as Jesus is entering Capernaum. The news of his return traveled fast and the crowd filled the meeting place to overflowing. In Mark 2, we read the account of four friends bringing their paralyzed friend to Jesus: "Some men came, bringing to him a paralytic, carried by four of them. Since they could not get him to Jesus because of the crowd, they made an opening in the roof above Jesus and, after digging through it, lowered the mat the paralyzed man was lying on. When Jesus saw their faith, he said to the paralytic, 'Son, your sins are forgiven'" (vv. 3-5).

Without any other way to gain access to Jesus, the four friends cut a hole in the roof in order to lower their friend safely to Jesus. Their visible initiative was powerful evidence of their invisible affection. What a marvelous metaphor for spiritual friendship. When we offer such intentional encouragement to one another, we are like those unnamed stretcher-bearers bringing their needy friend to the Lord.

The early church was filled with spiritual friends as well. By far the best example of oneness, unity and love among spiritual friends in the early church oc- cur during Pentecost. This fresh move- ment of the Holy Spirit drew these friends together and kept them from the divi- sions and obstacles Paul addressed throughout his ministry. In Acts, the out- pouring of the Spirit's power among spir- itual friends is a wonder to behold.

Barnabas had John Mark, the seven had each other to wait on the tables of over- looked widows (Acts 6), and Cornelius had his entire family. Paul had many spiri- tual friends, but in particular he had Barn- abas, the encourager, and Timothy, his son in the faith. Paul's journeys kept him in touch with many other friends. In Romans 16 he refers to Phoebe, Priscilla and Aqui- la, his relatives Andronicus and Junias, Tryphena and Tryphosa, just to name a few. He urges his spiritual friends "to watch out for those who cause divisions and put obstacles in your way that are con- trary to the teaching you have learned. Keep away from them. For such people are not serving our Lord Christ, but their own appetites" (Romans 16:17-18).

What did all of these people have in common? The active, undeniable pres- ence of the Holy Spirit, accompanied by the loving support of a caring commu- nity. The Spirit's peace transformed their experience from disarray to har- mony, from hopelessness to joy, from confusion to discernment. The way for- ward as friends was marked by the dis- cernible empowerment of the almighty One. The Spirit's power as reflected in the community of faith became trans- formational for all.

This is the paradigm for healthy com- munity. The Spirit is central to the vitality of all shared experiences in worship, work and witness. Without the empower- ment of God's Spirit, our spiritual friends would be mere acquaintances. In spiritu- al friendship there is heartfelt depen- dence on God. The Spirit releases within us the kind of honesty, transparency, lis- tening, accountability and sharing that we long for in our relationships, particu- larly within the context of our immediate Christian community.

Spiritual friendships come in different forms. They can form through relation- ships with our peers as well as with coaches, counselors, mentors, disciplers and pastors. They can be comprised of one-on-one relationships, triads, small groups and large groups. They form at different seasons of life and often are more meaningful during times of great need. No matter what our situation is, spiritual friends are gifts from God and are to be treated with respect, honor, gratitude and joy.

Who among us doesn't need a spiritual friend? The refreshment we experience when godly encouragement comes from the voice, hand and heart of a loving friend is like a pitcher of cold flowing wa- ter on a sweltering summer day. We have received such an outpouring from the Holy Spirit, and we are privileged to share and receive this gift with and from oth- ers. In the empowering presence of the Spirit and the covenantal love of a caring community we grow individually and to- gether in the Lord.

Without a doubt, we cannot become the people God intends for us to be without a community of friends surrounding us with gifts only they can offer. Spiritual friendship is a treasured commodity in the twenty-first century, and those who are in pursuit of their personal rule of life will need the encouragement, guidance and prayerful support of others. Leaning on those who know us best and love us most will enable us to reap great fruit for the glory of God throughout our faith-filled lives.

What is the state of your soul? This is the primary question explored in spiritual friendships and spiritual community. It's the question that takes us to the heart of the matter and focuses on what's going on in the deepest place within, where God alone seeks to reside (our soul), out of which all of life is fulfilled. When we have friends in community who are willing to go there with us, we plumb the depths and reside together in the midst of the nitty-gritty material of our lives. Authentic sharing opens the way to spiritual friendship where there is no need to compare, contrast, correct or contradict one another. We simply come alongside each other to bring out the very best of what God desires to create, redeem, sustain or transform in our everyday lives.

The context for our faith and our individual rule of life is our spiritual community. Within this community we share a common dependence on the ministry and movement of the Holy Spirit. But how do we care for one another's souls as spiritual friends?

First, we *love*. Like a cup of cold water in Jesus' name, we offer our friendship with sincerity, honesty and authenticity. In love, we offer earnest prayer for one another—not the kind that wants to fix, correct or change another's mind but prayer that comes from a posture of listening to each other and responding compassionately and empathically. By offering each other honest encouragement, we pour out compassion from the genuine reservoir of love within us, and thus our friend truly knows we are there for him or her no matter what.

Second, we *listen*. Spiritual friendship brings out the full story of people's lives. Humbly and intently, with great interest, accompanied by follow-up questions and very few interruptions, we listen carefully to how our friends' voices reflect what's truly going on inside. We listen for the call of God on their lives and fan that flame with gusto. Whenever possible, we listen at three levels: with an ear for (1) God's gentle voice, (2) the true voice of our friend and (3) the voice of invitation for us as listeners to respond to God's initiative. One of the greatest gifts of love is the willingness to carve out the time and space to be available to listen. When we are genuinely and intensely listened to by another, we know we are loved.

Third, we *learn*. We recognize that everyone is in the maturation process, coming to know Christ with ever increasing intimacy, learning the ropes of the Christian life, and continually submitting to the love and leadership of Christ. We learn best from God's Word, so when spiritual friends are in God's Word together, the Scriptures come alive in their hearing and bring hope and health to their relationship. We learn as well from the lives of others who have gone before us in church history, those who surround us today in the life of the church, and those who know us best and love us most. We learn too from our experiences, both the life-giving ones and the life-draining ones. When we come to understand that God wants to redeem every ounce of pain and heartache, as well as multiply every experience of joy and delight, we begin to recognize him more frequently in the everyday circumstances of our lives.

Fourth, we *lead*. Spiritual friends serve one another by leading their friends back to the center of their soul. It's here that the Savior resides, and when our conversations and shared experiences are enriched by the Spirit's presence, we end up back in the center of God's will. The deepest work of the Spirit often occurs at the place of repentance, reconciliation and renewal. As a result, we are invited back to joy, a state not dependent on circumstances. Joy occurs when the heart is inclined to the Spirit's invitation. Our rule of life is best understood, articulated and fulfilled with joy.

1. 1 Samuel 20 is a rich portrayal of the spiritual friendship that existed between Jonathan and David. As you reflect on this passage, what evidence do you see that Jonathan "loved [David] as he loved himself" (v. 17)?

2. Mark 2: 1-12 is the story of the four stretcher-bearers lowering their paralyzed friend to Jesus. What does this act of love and compassion say about their faith in Jesus?

3. Romans 12:9-21 is one of the apostle Paul's greatest descriptions of love among spiritual friends in community. What about this passage is most applicable to your current context of friendships?

Historical Insight

Do all the good you can,
By all the means you can,
In all the ways you can,
In all the places you can,
At all the times you can,
To all the people you can,
As long as ever you can.

—John Wesley's rule of life

In the history of the church there are few examples of godly leaders who model for us the priority of spiritual friendship within the community of faith better than John Wesley. Born on June 17, 1703, to Samuel and Susanna Wesley, John's life was remarkable from a very early age. In 1709, when John was six, he was rescued from a fire in the rectory and so called himself the "brand plucked from the burning." John received his education at the Charterhouse School in London and later went to Christ Church College in Oxford (1720-1724), where he earned his bachelor's degree. While studying at Oxford he steadily prepared for ordination, even though his heart was not entirely involved in his preparation.

In 1727 he was elected to a fellowship at Lincoln College at Oxford, where he earned his master's degree. Both John and his brother Charles were unsatisfied with their own spiritual state, as well as that of Oxford at large. So after serving alongside his father in the church, Wesley returned to Lincoln College and founded the Holy Club, a small group of men who "typically met privately in groups of 3 or 4 to pray, have devotional studies, and religious conversation. The emphasis was on good works, encouraging such practices as delivering medicines, Bibles, and tracts to the poor and needy, celebrating communion with prisoners, securing legal aid for the accused, and helping illiterate prisoners learn to read." The Holy Club served them by providing a place "to cultivate the life of prayer and sacrament and to sponsor serious reading."

Uncertain of his calling to succeed his father and unsatisfied with his life as a fellow at Lincoln College, Wesley

> still sought an ultimate authority and he believed that he had found it in the traditions and teachings of the early Church. Fundamentally the members of the Holy Club tried to return to the "ancient, if not apostolical" practices of the Church. This was where Wesley's own studies had persuaded him that the life commanded in the Scriptures was in practice carried out.

Wesley knew the gospel and that Christ died for the whole world, but did not yet know Christ as his own Savior. Wesley feared that he was "almost a Christian" and "not a whole Christian." Then on May 24, 1738, while Luther's preface to the epistle to the Romans was read in a public religious (Moravian) meeting, John Wesley was converted.

John Wesley devoted the rest of his life bringing back "the ideal of an apostolic, primitive church" to the contemporary Church of England.

He drew from primitive Christianity an ideal of what Christianity and the church should be. One of the primary ways that Wesley strove to bring the ideal of the apostolic, primitive church to the contemporary Church of England was through the Methodist Class Meetings. In his subsequent organization of the Methodist movement each local church was called a "Society" and within these societies there were numerous smaller groups of twelve or less people called a "Class." Each of the classes was under the authority of a Class Leader.

In a class meeting members would offer prayers, sing, and spur one another on to love and good works. The class members would give "brief accounts of their religious experience. Some of them, with deep sorrow, complained of 'the burden they felt because of their consciousness of the remains of 'indwelling sin.'"

If people wanted to officially join a Methodist Society, they needed a recommendation from their class leader after having gone to the class at least three times. Wesley thought this "filter" very important because it provided for the stability of the Societies. "The class meeting, the basic unit of Methodism, was a means of weekly examination and correction for members of the societies. Therefore, discipline was a key element in the Methodist movement."

Wesley instituted Methodist class meetings not as a replacement of church but as a complement. Class meetings empowered the laity and helped cultivate holy living apart from Sunday mornings. Wesley believed that the Church of England had "failed to bring their members into a close bond of religious union," and so the class meeting was established to remedy the deficiency.

Wesley's mother's instructions to him to "enter upon serious examination of yourself, that you may know whether you have a reasonable hope of salvation by Jesus Christ, that is, whether you are in a state of faith and repentance or not" was eventually translated into a series of questions to be asked at the weekly class meetings. In this way, "Wesley's practical divinity was accountability in community." Wesley believed that meeting together in a class was a means of grace. The format for a typical class meeting was (1) singing a short hymn, (2) the leader stating the condition of his soul/spiritual life and (3) the members testifying of the previous week's spiritual experience, including their victories and failures.

The Methodist society comprised all Methodists in a particular area, divided into classes of twelve. Each class had a leader who reported to the preacher in charge of the local society. The list of questions created by John to help class leaders in discussion were (1) What known sins have you committed since our last meeting? (2) What temptations have you overcome? (3) How did God deliver you? (4) What have you thought, said or done that might be sinful?

If repentant, the sinner was gladly invited back. If obstinate, says Wesley, "It was openly declared they were not of us. The rest mourned and prayed for them, and yet rejoiced, that, as far as in us law, the scandal was rolled away from the society." Referring to the class meeting, Henry Ward Beecher once commented, "The greatest thing John Wesley ever gave to the world is the Methodist class-meeting. And D. L. Moody once commented that the Methodist class-meetings are the best institution for training converts the world ever saw."

Class meetings brought people of different socioeconomic status together.

> The servant girl would follow her mistress in telling the people what God had done for her. The leader of the class might be the manager of the local factory or he might be one of the workingmen engaged there. The social grades were brought together to a common level, when each week, the people met together to pray, and praise, and share their experience.

It was not uncommon for class meeting groups to remain together for years; thus they developed intimate and edifying friendships.

> In this circle of companionship, it was difficult to be evasive or hypocritical. Deep levels of trust and affection were engendered: an optimum environment for the cultivation of personal character. Hearty thanksgiving and praise to God accompanied and affirmed every step of progress; loving and understanding, sympathy and encouragement, bolstered personal failures.

We owe a debt of gratitude to John Wesley for his visionary service to the body of Christ and his lifelong desire of pursuing spiritual community and developing healthy spiritual friendships. His model, although it seems somewhat wooden to today's church, is an excellent example of how fruitful the intentional gathering of small groups can be for the spiritual formation of individuals and faith communities. In similar contexts small groups of spiritual friends can meet today to share the state of their soul and personal rule of life.

Personal Rule of Life

As we've seen throughout this book, the more we reflect on the meaning of each segment of the personal rule of life, the more attentive we become to the ongoing invitations of the Lord in all areas of life. As you look back over the previous chapters it's time to bring it all together.

I've started the process of crafting a rule of life by approaching one major topic at a time, giving room to navigate your way through the biblical and historical texts, as well as integrating each theme into your personal life in the context of your spiritual community. I purposely used two charts as a starting point (see pages 76-77 to review your roles, gifts, desires, vision and mission, and pages 135-36 to review your spiritual, relational, physical, financial and missional priorities). Take some time now to return to these overviews, and prayerfully consider them one item at a time. Do each of these statements and themes reflect your current understanding of God's invitation for you during this season of your life? If so, then celebrate that by living out this rule of life both descriptively and prescriptively. If not, then take some time to retool these statements into more life-giving attributes and priorities. These two charts are the essence of your personal rule of life and need to be revisited on a regular basis.

The charts are the most straightforward way of thinking through one major issue at a time. But it's not necessarily the most creative way to express your uniquely articulated rule of life. If you are a "chart" person, then keep it as is; if not, then you might want to take some time to recraft your rule of life into a more creative design.

There are a variety of ways to portray your personal rule of life. The following are a few alternative suggestions to consider:

- Begin by weaving together your personal rule of life, prayerfully editing your life statements (roles, gifts, desires, vision, mission), as well as the matrix of particularities (your daily, weekly, monthly, quarterly and annual spiritual, relational, physical, financial and missional priorities). For the time being, you might wish to simply reflect on these two charts and see how God affirms what you've written down before taking these charts and reformatting them into other visual portrayals of your rule of life.

- When you're ready to take your charts and reformat them, consider crafting your personal rule of life in a pictorial form (for example, in the form of a tree, with the roots defined as your life statements, the trunk as your daily life, and the branches and fruit as the particulars of your life).

  - OR, if you prefer graphic illustrations, consider using a pie graph; a wheel and spoke imagery; interlocking circles, triangles or ovals; or dotted lines connecting various symbols. Be creative!

  - OR write a hymn, a poem, a narrative or an autobiographical story of how your personal rule of life is taking shape.

  - OR create a bulletin board of photos, words or sayings, so that your personal rule of life has visual appeal and provides an ongoing reminder of what matters most to you.

  - OR craft your rule as lists of your life statements and the particulars of the personal rule written out in a simple streamlined form, similar to Jonathan Edwards's "Resolutions" (see "Historical Insights" in chap. 6).

- Or design your own creative alternative for portraying your rule of life in a way that expresses your uniquely God-designed personality and approach to life.

As a rule of thumb, you are encouraged not to view your personal rule of life as a document set in stone! You are not tied to completing this assignment as if your life were a finished product. Instead, this should be seen as an ongoing, life-transforming process with daily discoveries, wonderful new blessings and exciting experiences in your journey along the path of life God has for you. All of these things will enlighten and shape your understanding of how God is at work in, through and around you.

The goal is always to mine the depths of each major area (roles, gifts, desires, vision and mission) and priority (spiritual, relational, physical, financial, missional) with the eyes of your heart wide open to see how God is at work. As you discover that he's continuously working in your life, you will delight in opportunities to love, understand, respond and serve him out of the context of your personal rule of life.

The appendix in the back of this book features four anonymous companions, offering composite stories of a true-to-life college student, young mom, pastor and business person. All of them have crafted their personal rule of life in the manner by which we have approached this topic throughout the book. Their overarching statements of roles, gifts, desires, vision and mission are provided for your review. In addition, the details of their spiritual, relational, physical, financial and missional priorities are spelled out. In addition, statements of their commitment to the body of Christ and their spiritual community are provided for your edification. Consult these examples as an encouragement for the completion of your own personal rule of life.

God bless you with the abundance of his grace, mercy and peace as you compile and craft your personal rule of life—an invitation to the well-ordered way!

Your personal rule of life is a holistic description of the Spirit-empowered rhythms and relationships that create, redeem, sustain and transform the life God invites you to humbly fulfill for Christ's glory.

Spiritual Community

1. In Mark 2: 1-12, we read about four friends who serve as stretcher-bearers for their paralytic friend. How have your friends taken initiative on your behalf by bringing you to (or back to) Jesus, either in their prayers, tangible advocacy, or words of challenge and/or encouragement?

2. What aspects of John Wesley's class-meeting model (singing, sharing of the condition of one's spiritual life, testimonies of the previous week's spiritual experience) are most appealing to you? Why? What ideas can you incorporate into your spiritual friendship group?

3. What are the characteristics or qualities of a spiritual friend that mean the most to you? What do you offer most often to others?

4. Spend time giving thanks in prayer for those spiritual friends who have come alongside you during critical seasons of life and have poured courage into your soul.

5. Close by sharing with one another the most recent version of your personal rule of life (begin with your life statements—roles, gifts, desires, vision and mission; then share one or more of your priority areas—spiritual, relational, physical, financial and missional). Listen for how each person has uniquely crafted their rule of life in ways that reflect God's thumbprint on their life. Affirm one another with prayers of thankfulness in each other's behalf.

Loving Father, my spiritual friends are by far some of the most precious gifts of my life. By name, I now wish to thank you, Lord, for each of them [pray for as many as come to your heart and mind]. May I continue to be a good friend to each life, practicing the priorities of attentiveness, hospitality, forgiveness, compassion and joy. May all of my friends grow in grace and wisdom as a result of being in relationship with me, receptible to the point of receiving you, Lord, the one who sent me to them for such a time and season as this. I love you, Lord, and I thank you for the many gifts that come from the generous hands of my friends. Help us all, by your grace, to continue to reflect our rule of life humbly and for your glory. In Christ's name. Amen.

LORD, you have assigned me my portion and my cup;
    you have made my lot secure.
The boundary lines have fallen for me in pleasant places;
    surely I have a delightful inheritance. . . .
You have made known to me the path of life;
    you will fill me with joy in your presence,
    with eternal pleasures at your right hand. (Psalm 16:5-6, 11)

CONCLUSION

An Invitation to the Well-Ordered Way

Therefore, I urge you, brothers, in view of God's mercy, to offer your bodies as a living sacrifice, holy and pleasing to God—this is your spiritual act of worship. Do not conform any longer to the pattern of this world, but be transformed by the renewing of your mind. Then you will be able to test and approve what God's will is—his good, pleasing and perfect will.

ROMANS 12:1-2

❖

Congratulations! You've done some fabulous work processing and praying your way through this interactive workbook. You've discerned from the Lord his loving invitation to intimacy as well as his intentions for your daily life and service to others. Don't lose sight of that as you seek to fulfill your personal rule of life.

The Father wants all his beloved children to know how best to follow his heart. The Lord of all ages is the lover of your soul, and the incredible love he has for you is an indication of how much he longs for your intimate fellowship. All you need to do is lean fully on him, rest secure in his love, and trust him with your heart, soul, mind and strength.

As you listen intently to his voice, you will discover on a daily basis that his call to this personal rule of life will enlighten your heart. That is a faith fact worth celebrating!

The reality is that before you started reading this text and praying your way through each chapter, you already had a rule of life in place. How you previously were utilizing your twenty-four hours each day was the embodiment of that rule. But now you've been introduced to biblical, historical and modern examples of those who discovered and pursued their God-ordained, Spirit-empowered, Christ-focused personal rule of life.

And you've seen that by living with prayerful intentionality they were remarkably transformed. Now it's your turn.

We all long to be in the center of God's delight and design. Out of a posture of growing awareness, we become people after God's own heart. It takes time, prayer, creativity, attentiveness and effort, but it is well worth the pursuit. When we linger in the reality of a trusting relationship with him, he whispers words of love and direction into our listening ears, words that define and delight us as his children. These are the words that create life in all its fullness: life from the inside out.

In celebrating our personal rule of life we are in essence celebrating God. Unless we learn to do so reflectively, we will remain manipulative. We need ongoing revision and review in order to keep our personal rule of life fresh. It's incumbent upon us to commit to a disciplined intentionality that will keep us in touch with God, our spiritual friends and our own heart. Then and only then will we experience heartfelt renewal.

We all want to get to the place where our personal rule of life is life-giving and energizing. Focusing on discovering God's great intentions for your life will best align with God's design for you as a uniquely created child of the King. He has assigned you your portion and your cup, he has made your lot secure. The boundary lines for you have fallen in pleasant places along a well-ordered way. Your path of life will be filled with joy in his presence and great delight in your inheritance, both in this life and for all eternity. Continue forward with prayerful discernment and determination, and don't settle for anything less than God's loving intentions for you!

> *Loving Father, my life is in your hands of mercy. I offer myself to you as a living sacrifice, with an earnest desire to be holy and pleasing in your sight. I know that this is my true and proper worship. Help me by your infinite grace to no longer pattern myself after the world's intentions for me, but instead be transformed by your loving invitation to renew my heart, soul and mind in accordance with your calling and delight. I long to be able to discern, understand and affirm your good, pleasing and perfect will for my life. Lead me onward in pursuit of your discernible intentions for me in every aspect of my personal rule of life. For the honor of your name, Father, Son and Holy Spirit, and the building up of your kingdom—now and forever. Amen.*

For additional information on crafting a personal rule of life, join the conversation and receive ongoing encouragement and practical resources from the Rule of Life online community at www.RuleOfLife.com.

RESOURCES FOR CREATING
A COMMUNAL RULE OF LIFE

A collective rule of life might be based on your congregation's shared covenant, vision and mission statements, or other church documents. Using any of these documents as a framework, invite the church leadership to prayerfully discern what shared practices and relational priorities define best your life together. Living intentionally around such a shared rule will deepen the worship, fellowship and witness of the people in response to God's ongoing call and movement in your midst. The following are suggested resources for expanding the concept of a personal rule of life into a community rule of life (the subject of another book!).

The Society of Saint John the Evangelist is a religious community of Episcopal monks. They have a community rule of life that's worth reviewing as you create your own personal rule or while crafting one for your spiritual community. This resource can be found online at www.ssje.org/audiorule.

New Life Fellowship in New York City has a community rule of life and suggestions for following the Daily Office. Their resources are based on *Emotionally Healthy Spirituality*, a book written by their pastor, Peter Scazzero. This resource can be found online at http://newlifefellowship.org/about.us/who-we-are/rule-of-life.

Local churches sometimes don't use the term *community rule of life* but may have a similar document, often called their "church covenant." There are many ways to craft a church covenant. Leadership Transformations has a helpful guide to follow for your local church. This resource can be found at www.leadershiptransformations.org/offer.htm.

Learning how to share from the heart and listen from the soul is a skill worth acquiring as a small group of spiritual friends. Two great books to get you started are *Spiritual Friendship* by Mindy Caliguire and *Seeking God Together* by Alice Fryling—both from InterVarsity Press (www.ivpress.com). Reflective readings and retreat resources on this subject from Leadership Transformations can be found at www.leadershiptransforma tions.org/store.

SUGGESTED READING
ON CHURCH HISTORY NOTABLES

Chapter 1: Roles

For more on C. S. Lewis's role as spiritual director and within the context of his own spiritual formation, read Lyle Dorsett's wonderful text, *Seeking the Secret Place: The Spiritual Formation of C. S. Lewis* (Grand Rapids: Brazos, 2004).

Chapter 2: Gifts

For more on Phillis Wheatley and her outstanding poetry, see Vincent Caretta's *Phillis Wheatley: Complete Writings* (New York: Penguin Classics, 2001).

Chapter 3: Desires

For more information about Harold J. Ockenga, consult Garth M. Rosell's *The Surprising Work of God* (Grand Rapids: Baker Academic, 2008).

Chapter 4: Vision

There are several translations of Benedict's Rule available to the modern day reader. In this book I have used *The Rule of Saint Benedict*, ed. Timothy Fry (New York: Vintage Books, 1998).

Chapter 5: Mission

An excellent resource which captures the mission and zeal of Adoniram Judson is Courtney Anderson's *To the Golden Shore: The Life of Adoniram Judson* (Valley Forge, Penn.: Judson Press, 1987).

Chapter 6: Time

Jonathan Edwards's *Religious Affections* is both readable and inspirational for the committed believer who wishes to study Edwards from the vantage point of personal spiritual vitality. See *The Works of Jonathan Edwards, Vol. 2: Religious Affections*, ed. John E. Smith (New Haven: Yale University Press, 2009).

Chapter 7: Trust

Two good biographies on William Wilberforce are Eric Metaxas's *Amazing Grace: William Wilberforce and the Heroic Campaign to End Slavery* (New York: HarperCollins, 2007), and John Pollock's *Wilberforce* (New York: St. Martin's Press, 1977).

Chapter 8: Temple

For more information about Augustine, consider reading Henry Chadwick's *Augustine of Hippo: A Life* (Oxford: Oxford University Press, 2009).

Chapter 9: Treasure

The fascinating life of George Mueller can be explored in more detail by reading one of the following texts: George Mueller, *A Narrative of Some of the Lord's Dealing with George Muller, Written by Himself* (Charleston, S.C.: BiblioBazaar, 2007), and George Mueller, *Autobiography of George Mueller: A Million and a Half in Answer to Prayer*, comp. G. Fred Bergin (Denton, Tex.: Westminster Literature Resources, 2003).

Chapter 10: Talent

For additional reflection on the life of Fanny Crosby, consult John Loveland's *Blessed Assurance: The Life and Hymns of Fanny J. Crosby* (Nashville: Broadman, 1978), or Fanny Crosby's autobiography *Memories of Eighty Years* (James H. Earle, 1906).

Chapter 11: Commitment to the Body of Christ

To know Calvin best, one must read his remarkable theological treatises, most notably his *Institutes of the Christian Religion*, trans. Ford Lewis Battles, 2 vols. (Louisville: Westminster John Knox Press, 2006).

Chapter 12: Spiritual Friendships

To better acquaint yourself with Wesley's approach to building community, read D. Michael Henderson's *John Wesley's Class Meeting: A Model for Making Disciples* (Nappanee, Ind.: Evangel Publishing House, 1997).

Four Individuals Crafting
Their Personal Rule of Life

In this section we will examine reflections from four companions who are also discerning and crafting a personal rule of life. Josh is a college student who's studying pre-law at a state university. Anne is a young mom trying to balance the growing demands on her time at home and in the community. Mike is a pastor of a growing church in the Midwest. Lynn is a type-A business executive who's continually challenged by her desire to live a balanced life but keeps adding more and more to her already filled plate.

Each of these companions represent real people who have attended personal rule-of-life training events where I have interacted with their stories and helped them identify life-giving rhythms and relationships that have created, sustained, redeemed and transformed their lives. Though the names are fictitious, the data is real. These stories are included to serve as an encouragement as you formulate your own statements. But as you refer to their stories, it's best to remain open to God's specific work in your life. Avoid the temptation to copy what these companions have created for their own personal rule.

College Student (Josh)

Roles. "Although I'm feeling pretty good about my current relationships and the number of roles I'm carrying this semester, I sense the need to join a small group. I've been pushing hard to complete my junior year and realize that I've been neglecting to establish some long-term friendships while still at college. The InterVarsity staff person lives down the hall and has been inviting me to join his group for the past two years; it's time I do so. Another area that needs some attention is my relationship with my girlfriend. We're getting along OK, but I know we're avoiding some important issues that keep coming up. I'm willing to go there, but I'm not sure she is. It's really in my lap to figure out how to bring these up and address them honestly. I want to know if this is the woman for me. Finally, I've definitely been ignoring my parents these days, and it seems like each time we're on the phone or together in person we're at each other's throats. We keep going back to all the old patterns of our relationship that bug me the most. I'm sensing that God wants me to reach out to them more often, so I'll try and do that each week of my junior year and see how that helps."

Some of Josh's roles include *believer* (in relationship with God), *son* (in relationship with his mother, stepfather and father); *brother* (to his three older siblings), *student* (at the state university), *small group leader* (for his life group on campus), *barista* (at the local coffee shop), and *friend* (to his girlfriend and others on campus)

Gifts. "Last summer I took one of those spiritual gifts inventories, but I'm still not very clear about what mine are today. Some of my friends have suggested that I have the gift of partying and basketball, but I don't see either of those listed in the Bible! In all seriousness, I would like to think that I have the gift of teaching since I really enjoy getting ready to teach almost any subject, when given the opportunity. I sure hope I have the gift of leadership, because my whole direction here in college is toward getting a management job in the workplace when I graduate. I've enjoyed each of my part-time and summer jobs (even picturing myself being "in charge" and projecting how I'd lead differently than my bosses; I think I had some much better ideas than they did, if I do say so myself!). Besides those two gifts, I know I enjoy leading worship and playing my guitar with my buddies; we love to practice together each Sunday night at the student union. I'm trusting that I'll be able to hone my gifts and abilities while I'm still in school and look forward to using them for God in the future."

Some of Josh's gifts, talents and temperament: *gifts* are teaching and leadership; *talents* include leading worship, hospitality and photography; still learning about *temperament* and what makes him tick positively and what ticks him off negatively.

Desires. "When I think about what matters most to me, I can't help but remember my grandfather, who used to sit with us on the front porch after dinner and talk with us about his views on everything—sports, family, work, chores, studies, politics and religion. We bombarded him with questions and loved listening to him speak about the "good ol' days" when life was simpler, values were upheld and everyone knew each other. With the incredible growth of technology, and with the globalization and urbanization and the distance between generations that now exists, it's hard to know what we share in common. I guess what I've learned is that Christian values should guide my life. I'm still not sure what that means, exactly, but I hope to discover more about what I really value most as I continue to study in college. But when asked what I'm passionate about, I definitely know that I believe in justice, freedom, human rights and the importance of caring for the poor and the "least of these." I hope that as I move out of this stage of life and into the real world, I can concentrate some of my energies on pursuing these passions with focus and intentionality. Not sure how, but I'm pretty convinced I know why."

Vision. "I'm pretty sure I know some of the parts of my vision, but I recognize too that my age is most likely leading me into a more naive sense of my future. I've been

Chart 1

JOSH	TIME	TRUST	TEMPLE	TREASURE	TALENT
Daily	Quiet time of prayer and Bible study	Time with girlfriend and buddies at school.	Groom and eat right!	Always have a few bucks in my pocket!	Keep up with studies!
Weekly	Attend and serve at church	Call home and keep up relationship with Mom, Dad and sibs; lead small group.	Work out @ gym 4x/week Pick up b-ball at least 1x/ week	Deposit pay check Give something to church	Keep up with PT job!
Monthly		Reach out to grandparents, and at least one of my aunts, uncles, cousins.	Look back and confess sins to clean up temple!	Reconcile credit card and other bills with bank account	Keep up discerning God's will for my life!
Quarterly	Soul sabbath with other students from InterVarsity chapter on campus		One "push myself" bike ride or jog or swim		
Annually	Retreat with buddies	Family reunion; vacation with buddies and possibly parents and sibs; home for holidays; remember bdays!	Get to doc and dentist!	Take over paying my taxes!	By this time next year, have a completed resume and plan for future!

asking God to clarify what his vision is for me, and all I think I hear is to wait and trust and keep my eyes open for what's ahead. But with all that I'm studying here at college, my heart and mind keep going to using my business degree to help build a company or a nonprofit organization that will make a difference for others who are more needy than the average American. I now think my vision will include something about God using me as his instrument for justice and peace. Maybe as a layperson in a church or as a leader in the marketplace or taking on some role in our community. So, for now I'm leaning toward a vision statement that includes God's call to work for peace and justice, most likely in needy parts of the United States or in a developing country. I don't feel called to the really difficult places (maybe I'm just too afraid) but feel led to a leadership role of some kind in a place that's creative, energizing and productive."

Josh's first attempt at a vision statement: I long to be free to be myself in Christ. I long to be a conduit for the Holy Spirit for the sake of others. I long to interact with those in front of me based only on my love for God and my love for them.

Mission. Since Josh is studying pre-law at the university and hopes to some day either work for or start a nonprofit organization, his mission statement might include (1) doing his best in school and taking courses that might help him in the future to pursue his vision, (2) possibly taking a summer internship at a nonprofit to see if this is really what God is leading him toward, (3) seeing if his girlfriend is excited about this, and (4) enjoying his college years to the fullest as a unique time for fellowship and growth.

Proposed mission statement. To study and discover the best vocational path for me to pursue postcollege, to prayerfully consider proposing to my girlfriend, and to pursue every possible option for growing as a leader and man of God.

Commitment to the body of Christ. "My commitment to the body of Christ . . . I know that church is important but it's really hard right now to see beyond just the weekly worship services I attend. I need to learn more about the wider body of Christ and stretch my understanding of the many different denominations today. I'm not really sure how they all came into being, but I am curious to learn more. With my background, I can't help but believe I'll be a part of the church for my entire life. I hope that no matter where I live, there will be a great church to join."

Spiritual community. "My spiritual community . . . right now my small group is one of the best parts of my week. These guys would do anything for me (and vice versa) and I know that what I share with them will be held in strict confidence. I will always be in a small group and hope that I'll be able to facilitate the kind of community we currently enjoy together each week. These are by far the best friends I've ever had. I'll keep maintaining these kinds of friendships forever."

Young Mom (Anne)

Roles. "I'm exhausted! That's about all I know these days. With two preschoolers constantly nipping at my ankles, I'm spent to the max. So, when I think about my roles, number one is mom, and that will be true for a long time. But this means that my husband and I need to spend more blocks of time together, and we've been trying to make that happen. With this personal rule of life exercise, I'm realizing that I want this more than I've given voice to recently. We need to make this a weekly priority. Also, I'm really enjoying my moms' study group each week but have come to the decision that I can't volunteer for any of the additional service opportunities they make available to us. So, that's a no for sure. I need these girlfriends and my mentor now more than ever, so I'm committed to staying in this group each week. I've not seen my parents recently and need to make that happen at least quarterly; the five-hour drive really shouldn't keep me home, especially since their age and physical condition keeps them from traveling our direction. If I can swing it, I'd like to take an online course to keep my nursing career on track for the day I return to working at the hospital after my youngest goes to kindergarten."

Some of Anne's roles include *wife* (to husband John), *mom* (to two preschoolers), *friend* (to as many young moms as her calendar can handle!), *daughter* (to her aging parents), *sister* (to her two siblings), *child of God* (desirous of growing in her faith), and *volunteer* (although trying to cut down on too many irons in the fire).

Gifts. "When I was a child, I remember pretty clearly how much I loved to play with my dolls, pretend and imagine with my doll house, build tents (that served as homes) with sheets, blankets, pillows and stuffed animals in our family room. My friends in the neighborhood joined me in this creative play, and we knew someday we'd be moms and wives. I know without a shadow of a doubt that my greatest gifts and calling in life center around the home. My husband and children are my priority, so I hope that my primary gift is hospitality. I'm pretty committed to making memories, enjoying each season of our children's lives and preparing them for their life after the nest. My temperament feeds into this longing of my heart, and I suppose my talents do too. I'm pretty sure that someday I'll have to return to the workplace to help with college bills and the more expensive time of family life. But in the meantime, I'm content to remain focused on my home and family. Outside the home, I enjoy helping other young moms, and I volunteer on occasion at the church. But I don't have much additional time to offer elsewhere. My gifts and talents are needed most in our home, and I assume God is pleased with my attention here."

Some of Anne's gifts, talents and temperament: *Gift* of hospitality is primary; role of motherhood is augmented by her *talent* in creating a home that's nurturing, safe and loving; she's pretty self-assured having come from a healthy home herself, so her *temperament* is ideal for raising young children with patience, grace and creativity.

Desires. "My core values spring forth from my family heritage. Having been raised in a Christian family and in a biblically based church, I learned from an early age what it means to pursue godly family values. I recall with tenderness the times we spent with cousins and extended family. But there was a residual tension in our immediate family that I have yet to fully understand. My parents were highly regarded in the community, having jobs that kept them in touch with leaders and townspeople. But on the home front we lacked the kind of unity and oneness that we as kids longed for all our lives. So, when we got married and started our own family, we set out to break some old patterns and establish priorities that meant the most to us. Therefore, I must say I'm renewed in my excitement to raise our children in ways that bless them, bring out the best in them and as a result provide for us great joy in our shared journey. We want our home to be a household of faith, just like we promised each other on our wedding day. I'm pretty passionate about that, especially when I hear stories from my girlfriends about their families of origin and how they struggle to understand how best to raise their own children. I certainly don't have a handle on it myself, but we're committed to pursuing healthy family life to the best of our ability."

Vision. "When I think of the word *vision* I can hardly think beyond today! Being a young mom is taxing in and of itself. My vision is wrapped around what our family will become in the future and specifically how well the children will do as they grow older. I guess you could say that my vision is to be the kind of mom that fosters growth in her household—and faith, love, joy and peace too. I love my life as a mom and I trust that my life will matter most when all is said and done, as my kids mature and ultimately live independently and have families of their own. In addition to my children, I want to be a good wife to my husband, a good friend to others and a faithful servant of the Lord as a neighbor and supporter of the needy. When I consider the end of my life (kind of a gruesome thought, I might add), my hope is that I'll be remembered as a person who was willing to go the extra mile for others. I really enjoy some of my volunteer work these days and trust that will continue for many more years. All in all, my vision is to be a godly woman and to discover as many ways as possible to bring out the best in others."

Anne's first draft of a vision statement: My heart's desire is to be known as a loving wife, gentle mother, generous friend and patient servant of God. Like Jesus, I want to bring out the best in others who surround me in life.

Mission. With Anne's obvious focus on her immediate family at this season of life, her personal mission statement will deal primarily with her roles as wife and mother. Some of the emphasis will include friendships and volunteering in a few settings, but with young children needing her ongoing attention, her missional priorities will rightfully focus on her family. It's important that Anne also be encouraged to take good care of herself, since she has acknowledged that her personal well being has ripple effects on the health of her family. Getting the rest she needs, alone time to regroup, friendships that restore her joy and date nights with her husband are included in this regard.

Probable mission statement. To be healthy enough myself—spiritually, relationally and physically—in order to lovingly care for the needs of my husband and family, while remaining available to serve others in Jesus' name.

Commitment to the body of Christ. "My commitment to the body of Christ . . . I'm not sure where I would be without the churches I've attended and been a part of nearly all my life. So I guess you might say I'm pretty committed to membership in a local church no matter where we live. I have experienced both the highs and lows of church life and realize there is no such thing as a perfect church. But at this season of our life as a fam-

Chart 2

ANNE	TIME	TRUST	TEMPLE	TREASURE	TALENT
Daily	Start day with prayer; read Bible with kids	Attentiveness to husband and children; awareness of their needs; personal space as needed	Fix nourishing meals; drink lots of water; eight hours of sleep if possible!	Categorize all purchases (keep receipts)	Be the best wife and mom I can be for my family!
Weekly	Family to church!	Moms group; talk with mentor; time with a friend	Get a run in 4x/week	Tithe to church; make sure kids have $$ for offering too	Keep reading books and magazines to keep my mind stimulated
Monthly	Bi-monthly moms' group and couples' study group	Mom's day off! Bi-monthly date nights	Walk with friend on wood trail or along ocean	Willingly and joyfully review credit card bill with husband.	Do something creative—concert, movie, paint, etc.
Quarterly					
Annually	Women's retreat	Make holidays special; family vacations; birthday joy	Dentist 2x/year; annual physical; Take kids for checkups too!	Help with tax return.	Keep ahead of what needs to be done around the house and tackle one project at a time

ily there is no other option for us. We want to raise our children in a God-fearing congregation and will do so for our entire lives."

Spiritual community. "My spiritual community . . . thankfully, God has given me some wonderful friends who are also young moms. We have forged a bond with one another that's unique and beautiful. We're there for each other no matter the need or the time of day. It's great to know that no matter what I'm facing in my day I can pick up the phone and find an empathetic ear. I'm looking forward to how these friendships will continue to grow in Christ."

Ministry Leader (Mike)

Roles. "Ever since the new building was completed, we've been trying to find our equilibrium as a staff team. We put so much on hold for nearly eighteen months that I'm pretty challenged by the task of figuring out what needs my greatest attention. As a result, I've decided to put together a weekly staff time where we can meet in triads and discuss how best to garner our resources and rebuild our relationships for the future of our church. This seems to be preoccupying my attention these days. Beyond that, I'm trying my best to be a good husband and father, but realizing through this exercise that my family has gotten the short end of the stick. My desire is for my wife and I to get back to 'dating' again, and I'm hoping that can happen sooner than later. Saturday mornings seem to work best for the kids, so instead of attending the men's breakfast group I'll start taking one or all the kids out for a fun meal and then run some errands or play together. I'm also hoping to find a spiritual director to process my prayer life. And it would be great if I could get back to fishing this summer with my college roommates who have been hoping I'd return for longer than I care to admit."

Some of Mike's roles include *Christian* (beginning with what should be top priority relationship—with God), *husband* (to his wife), *father* (to their two children), *pastor* (overseeing the staff team, working with the elders, counseling, preaching and teaching each week), *friend* (to small accountability group and with a handful of friends who he plays golf with and meets on occasion at the local gym), *volunteer* (in local soup kitchen with other pastors from the community once per month), and *brother* (to estranged siblings; parents died when he was in college).

Gifts. "With the growth of the church over the past few years, I'm realizing that my need as a pastor is to focus on the gifts that God has given to me, and not dwell on the ones I don't have (which can be so easy to do when I daydream and compare myself with others, particularly the more successful pastors I know nationally or in our region). I've taken some of the spiritual gifts inventories over the years and I come out strong on leadership, preaching and teaching. Since I'm spending the majority of my time exercising those gifts, I often come across as cold and demanding. What I need to confront within myself is my need to control and my propensity toward anger. Instead, I want to develop a team approach to ministry and build up others to balance my gifts and temperament so that the church is not hindered in our shared effectiveness. As a result, I need to let go of many of the tasks currently on my desk and delegate meaningful work to others. As I've prayed about this, I realize that I can often be the number one roadblock here. But if I lean into my gift of leadership, hopefully God will help me to be discerning and then invite other staff and lay leaders into the center of church leadership. I will need a lot of patience with others and myself in this process."

Some of Mike's gifts, talents and temperament: Mike has good self-awareness of his primary *gifts* of leadership, preaching and teaching; he's keen on the *talents* he possesses, including team building and outreach; regarding *temperament*, he's becoming aware of his propensity to control others and to have high expectations for everyone around him, beginning with himself.

Desires. "I've spent the majority of my adult life to date focused on the local church. As a teenager, when I invited Jesus into my heart, I began to see with growing clarity what was right about our church and what was sorely missing. When I sensed the call to full-time ministry, I knew that my passion was focused almost exclusively on church life. I tend to see most things through that lens. Our marriage and family life are best built around the church community. Our growing up in Christ happens supremely through the programs of the church. Our friends are here, our life is here, and our service to others is generated from this place. I guess what I'm coming to grips with is that my life is church-centered. I hope it's more Jesus centered than church-centered, because it's from the Lord that I have developed my own love for the church, the bride of Christ. I know others don't necessarily see life from this vantage point, but I hope to instill this mindset within my family and congregation. I love the church and I want to learn more and more how to love the church as Christ loves his bride, with sacrificial love and commitment. My passion, values, longings and goals center around this priority. I exist for the sake of building up God's kingdom through the local church."

Vision. "*Vision.* Sometimes the word excites me and other times it frightens me! But, really, I'm a visionary (or so they say), so when all is said and done I like to think about vision. But when it comes to being a visionary for myself I have a harder time. Most likely this is due to the fact that I tend to consider the word [vision] for our ministry and not for myself. I like how we're given permission to consider vision here; it's very freeing for a guy like me. My vision includes all my key roles as a husband, father, pastor, friend, volunteer and Christ follower. It certainly encompasses my passion for life and my zest for serving others in Jesus' name. When I dream about the future, my heart and mind tend to go toward what the church will become, but really it's more about where I want to grow. I long to be a man after God's own heart, just like the biblical characters I seek to emulate. My favorites are guys like King David and the apostle Paul, men like Stephen and even Zechariah. But sometimes I find myself relating to leaders like Jonah, who cares more about 'my own agenda' than truly following after God's. I guess that's what it's all about—having a vision for myself that comes more from God than from my best and brightest ideas."

Mike's first sketch of a vision statement: My vision is to become a man of the Father's heart, reflecting God's truth in my mind, revealing the Spirit in all my attitudes, and Jesus in all actions.

Mission. As we've discovered from Mike's previous reflections, his missional focus is on the local church where he serves as pastor. Both his philosophy of life and ministry, as well as his theological convictions, move him toward a central role of the local church for all aspects of life as a believer. This is honorable, but since it's not always realistic for others, his mission statement is designed to invite his family and congregation to consider this as well. His obvious love for God and the church is contagious, and his hope is that he will be able to positively influence those within his care to embrace the essence of his ministry and mission.

Projected mission statement. To embody the love of God—Father, Son and Holy Spir-

Chart 3

MIKE	TIME	TRUST	TEMPLE	TREASURE	TALENT
Daily	Time alone with God; practice new disciplines	1-on-1 space with wife; 1 family meal/ day; manage by walking around (MBWA) at office	Rise at 6 a.m.; get sleep too; physical activity in a.m.; healthy food in moderation	Keep watch on spending per category	Preaching and teaching prep . . . ongoing; pay attention to staff!
Weekly	Church; worship; family; sabbath	Date night! Kids hour! Saturday a.m. pancakes	Run, play soccer or other exercise 3x/ week	Tithe gross pay to church and other ministries	Staff meetings— individual meetings with key folks; weekly team meetings
Monthly	Pastor's prayer group; see spiritual director	Pastors round-table group; bi-monthly men's fellowship		Pay bills; reconcile bank statements	Board meetings— keep to two-hour-max agenda
Quarterly	Attend pastors conference	Hike with friend	Adjust exercise plan according to weather— add ocean swimming in summer	Discuss selling parsonage so our family can create equity	Team retreats to be determined
Annually	Two-day silent retreat	Family vacation; bday specials	Wilderness trip; new competitive sport?	Taxes; housing allowance amount	Annual performance reviews for all, including me with the board

it—teach the mission of God—in worship, love and service—and invite others into the kingdom of God and the church of the living God.

Commitment to the body of Christ. "My commitment to the body of Christ . . . Since church is so much a part of the essence of my life, I'm committed for the long haul. The network we are a part of provides all the resources we'll ever really need as a congregation and for us as a pastor's family. My seminary years solidified my belief in the priority of the local church, theologically, relationally and practically in the fulfillment of God's mission on earth. I'm excited to participate in continuing the legacy of church history for the years I'm a minister of the gospel."

Spiritual community. "My spiritual community . . . as much as I'd like to say I have spiritual friendships, I must admit that most of my relationships have a purposeful or functional intention to them. I long to see a handful of my buddies make a more consistent commitment to each other so we can grow deeper together, pray and support one another in our respective lives and ministries. I trust the Lord will open this door in the coming months."

Business Person (Lynn)

Roles. "I can already tell this personal rule of life exercise is going to mess up my world. There's no way I can keep up with fifteen major roles. My life has gotten seriously out of control. I'm not happy in any of them these days. My boss is always disgruntled with my work. My colleagues are driving me crazy. This ridiculous commute is sending my blood pressure through the roof. I have no time to take care of myself, never mind the demands that are growing at home. My drivenness is getting the best of me, and I feel trapped inside a cage of mice all competing for their turn on the wheel of endless motion heading nowhere fast. I really need to pull the plug and take a much-needed vacation. Help! OK, in all seriousness, I know I need to get to church each week no matter what's in my briefcase calling for my attention. I want to do more cooking each week. So, if my husband and I can get our act together, and if he is willing to do the grocery shopping, I'm sure I can pull off at least three meals per week. If I get up on time I'm really sensing the need to pray and read the Word, even if it's just an extended time over the weekend. Finally, if we can afford it, it's time we spent at least two weeks on vacation this summer. Maybe then I can figure out how to get my life back in order."

Some of Lynn's roles (not all fifteen!) include *wife* (to her husband of fifteen years), *mom* (to her only child, who's now in elementary school), *sister* (to a disabled brother and a sister, who lives in Europe), *daughter* (to parents in assisted living), *business executive* (at a downtown Fortune 100 firm), *church board member* (deacon board), and *athlete* (avid tennis player)

Gifts. "With the pace I'm living these days, and the demanding business that occupies me almost 24/7, it's hard not to notice my gifts being employed in a variety of settings. By far my greatest gift is discernment. I can see right into and through and beyond most issues. Some have called it wisdom or exhortation, but I prefer discernment. I also see that leadership or management or both (I'm not sure if management is a spiritual gift or a talent!) are a part of the core of my being. Where I struggle is in the areas of mercy or compassion. I'm not at all inclined in those directions (unfortunately). Since I can get so much done in sometimes lightening speed, I suppose I have a learned talent of efficiency. In most settings of my life, I'm also striving to become more effective, which I hope will slow me down internally and offset my drivenness. When I take the time to pray about my work, I end up feeling more convicted about my temperament than my gifts or talents. It's my temperament that executes and sometimes exhausts or frustrates others. That's where I need the most work in developing my personal rule of life. I will be reading more about the fruit of the Spirit and the beatitudes, since I'm convinced I'll find much to chew on in those passages that I hope will impact my temperament as a believer."

Some of Lynn's gifts, talents and temperament: Lynn's self-awareness will help her deal with the issues she's seeking to address, particularly in the area of temperament. If she can slow down enough, this can be a fertile exercise for her soul. Her *gifts* of leadership, wisdom and exhortation are obvious. Her *talents* of management and efficiency need to be complemented by a more patient and Christlike *temperament*, which she obviously desires.

Desires. "People in every setting of my life call me passionate. I guess it's because I am! I get all stirred up about most areas of my life because I'm so committed to every aspect of my existence—my work, my family, my church, my community. Isn't that the way it's supposed to be for everyone? There are so many times in my day when I look around and wonder where the passion is for others? I see more ho-hum, status quo, never change attitudes, and it drives me crazy at times. Life is to be lived to the fullest, and I'm constantly in motion because I believe every aspect of my life is to be lived to the fullest. I have little patience for others who don't see it this way. It kind of irks me when I'm not in a good mood, but it enlivens me when I'm in that 'good space' to make a significant difference and challenge those around me to embrace a higher standard of excellence. I'm passionate about my work; I love my job. I enjoy every aspect of my work, and when I hit projects that don't appeal to me, I try and delegate them to others. I like to stay focused; it helps me be productive. On the home front, I like things in good order, so I work hard to make that happen. And when I'm volunteering my time or resources, I really like to see multiplication in the lives of others who benefit most from the services rendered in their behalf."

Vision. "In my business setting, we tend to talk a lot about vision for our company and our employees, but seldom about ourselves. We operate as a team, therefore what we do collectively is far more important that what we accomplish as individuals. But on a daily basis I see how we can all get self-absorbed in reaching our goals and striving for excellence and climbing whatever ladder is standing in front of us. I'm guilty of this more times than I care to admit. So, as I pause for a while and sit with this question for myself, I'm drawn to a lot of passionate priorities that concern me deeply. I want to be a faithful follower of Jesus, I certainly desire to care for my husband and family. And it's pretty obvious that I want to be a successful business leader too. I've spent so much time, money and effort on these roles, and the accomplishments speak for themselves, if I must say so myself. Vision for me personally includes becoming the best I can be in all areas of my life. I guess that's why so many around me call me "driven"—must mean that I care about a lot of things going well at the same time, lots of plates spinning at once. But is that really my long-term vision? Not really. I want things to slow down so I can really discover what real living looks like."

Lynn's first crack at a vision statement: I long for my life to be balanced amidst the tensions of work, home, church, friendships and extended family. I want to be successful in my business endeavors for the glory of God and the good of others. If possible, I'd love to speak and write about what I'm learning in life.

Mission. Lynn is a competent, gifted, enthusiastic Christian in the marketplace. This world needs many more professionals like Lynn who love God and are committed to excellence in their work. She is to be commended for her hard work and her devotion to her company. As she's openly shared thus far in her reflections, she's trying to balance

Chart 4

LYNN	TIME	TRUST	TEMPLE	TREASURE	TALENT
Daily	Bible reading and prayer; try new devotional	Dinner—no matter what time—with family!	Stop eating pizza! Eat more salads! Drink more water!	Limit credit card use	Daily e-news and stock reports; daily in-house memos
Weekly	Church with family; fast one meal/week for our adopted orphan	Out to lunch with friend; prayer group on Friday a.m.	Exercise daily at gym; limit alcohol intake	Gift to church	Keep reading articles and newspapers and books!
Monthly	Review spiritual goals; read one Christian book	Husband time! Shopping with kids	Fast one full day/month	Pay all bills in timely fashion; monthly tithe to church and missions	Senior staff in-house mtgs; key customers for attention to client needs
Quarterly	Day at the ocean or hike in the woods to connect with God the Creator!	Weekend away—alone or with friends or husband		Projects completed around the house; invest in this our #1 investment!	Staff reviews and projections; personal projections/ goals
Annually	Attend church retreat	Super vacation; see extended family	Physical exams; be sure family gets exams!	Tax returns completed	Performance evaluations; compensation review; annual reports written

the tensions of seeking to be fully present and effective in every area of her life. This is something she'll continue to pursue as her career and family continue to grow. Her need for an older, wiser mentor will emerge and hopefully be fulfilled. In the meantime, her mission flows from her personhood and into her home and workplace.

Possible mission statement. It is my intention to pursue wholeness and balance within the very real tensions created by the pursuit of excellence in my walk with God, my love for family and my devotion to serve Christ in the workplace.

Commitment to the body of Christ. "My commitment to the body of Christ . . . I know the church is important, but there have been many times in my life that I have believed it's one of those nonessentials for our faith. I don't see in the Bible anything that looks like the churches I've attended recently. I can be a Christian and raise a believing family without regularly entering a church building. I guess I have a lot to learn about the importance of the church building and the need for us to gather there so regularly; I'm delighted to take a Sunday off and go to the ocean with my family or enjoy some sabbath rest on my own."

Spiritual community. "My spiritual community . . . I'm not sure what this really even means. I have lots of acquaintances and a handful of friends. But at this stage of my life the majority of my friends are work associates, and I hope that they see a smidgen of Jesus in me. My husband and children are my priority, so maybe we need to become more of that kind of community for each other. We definitely need to pray and read the Bible more together."

ACKNOWLEDGMENTS

I'm especially thankful to Ruthie, Nate and Bekah for their tireless encouragement and provision of unspeakable joy in our shared journey of faith and family life.

In addition, I am profoundly grateful to the Lord for the prayerful support received for this project by the Leadership Transformations board and ministry team. The incredibly life-giving Pierce fellows at Gordon-Conwell Theological Seminary, members of our Spiritual Leadership Community and our Selah interns have all joined me in wrestling with the concepts described in these pages and have faithfully written and shared their personal rule of life in my presence.

I'm particularly thankful for the grace-filled support of Garth Rosell and Dave Currie, and for their church history expertise. I'm also thankful for Alex Kirk, John Pryor and especially Kevin Antlitz as they assisted in advising and researching the church history notables.

Special kudos to Cindy Bunch and Bob Fryling for their visionary leadership at InterVarsity Press and their encouragement about the importance of this book.

To God alone belongs all the glory, honor and praise.

NOTES

Introduction: Crafting a Personal Rule of Life

p. 14   "What do you think of when you hear": David Vryhof, "Monastic Wisdom for Everyday Living," *Cowley Magazine* 37, no. 4 (2011).

Chapter 1: Roles

p. 23   Benner's five interrelated elements: David Benner, *Sacred Companions: The Gift of Spiritual Friendships and Direction* (Downers Grove, Ill.: InterVarsity Press, 2002)., p. 65-78.

p. 29   "May it be the real I who speaks": C. S. Lewis, *Letters to Malcolm: Chiefly on Prayer* (New York: Harcourt, 1991), pp. 109, 103, respectively.

p. 29   C. S. Lewis became a spiritual guide: Lyle W. Dorsett, *Seeking the Secret Place: The Spiritual Formation of C. S. Lewis* (Grand Rapids: Brazos, 2004), p. 110.

p. 29   "I cannot learn to love my neighbor as myself": C. S. Lewis, *Mere Christianity* (New York: HarperCollins, 2001), p. 87.

p. 29   "Lewis' ability to treat each letter writer with dignity": Dorsett, *Seeking the Secret Place*, pp. 120-21.

Chapter 2: Gifts

p. 35   "In truth, we cannot become anything other": Arthur F. Miller Jr. and William D. Hendricks, *The Power of Uniqueness: How to Become Who You Really Are* (Grand Rapids: Zondervan, 1999), p. 98.

p. 35   discovering our gifts is a rather straightforward process: Some of the assessments available online to consider using: "Gifted2Serve" can be accessed via BuildingChurch.net; the "Spiritual Gifts Analysis" can be accessed via ChurchGrowth.org; the "Spiritual Gifts Inventory" can be accessed via mintools.com; or search for others via "Online Spiritual Gifts Inventory, Assessment, Tool or Survey."

p. 35   there are many resources available to us: Some of these tools include the Myers-Briggs Temperament Indicator (MBTI), the Enneagram, MMPI and DISC.

p. 38   "Apparently quite brilliant and with an aptitude for learning": Omofolabo Ajayi-Soyinka, "A Conversation with Phillis Wheatley," in *History Alive! Study Guide* (Topeka: Kansas Humanities Council, 1995), pp. 3-5.

p. 39   "publishers in Boston had refused to publish the text": Ibid., p. 5.

Chapter 3: Desires

p. 45   "The opposite of wasting your life": John Piper, *Don't Waste Your Life* (Wheaton, Ill.: Crossway, 2007), p. 43.

p. 48   "Peter's pastoral commission flows out of": Pheme Perkins, *Peter: Apostle for the Whole Church* (Minneapolis: Fortress, 2000), pp. 183-84.

p. 48   " 'to attend strictly to duty,' to 'take all disappointments graciously' ": Garth M. Rosell, *The Surprising Work of God* (Grand Rapids: Baker Academic, 2008), p. 40.

p. 48   his life was yet to be completely transformed: Ibid., p. 41.

p. 49   "I covenanted with God that if he would save me": Ibid., p. 43.

p. 49   Taylor University Evangelistic Team: Ibid., p. 46.

p. 49   "prayer, fellowship, and mutual edification": Ibid.

p. 49   "an assured degree, an assured Fellowship": Ibid., p. 58.

p. 49   "often thrown together at youth rallies, revival meetings": Ibid., p. 118.

p. 49   "by the mid-1940s a recognizable 'band of brothers' ": Ibid., p. 119.

p. 50   Graham spoke to over 1.5 million people: Ibid., p. 153.

p. 50   *reclaim the culture* and *renew the mind*: Ibid., p. 196.

p. 50   "We are experiencing the mercy drops of God's blessings": Ibid., p. 84.

p. 50   Ockenga was absorbed in revival literature and history: Ibid.

p. 50   "All progress in Christian things is made by revivals": Ibid.

p. 50   He knew America needed revival: Ibid., p. 85.

Chapter 4: Vision

p. 59   "Fifteen hundred years ago, a young man studying in Rome": Timothy Fry, ed., *The Rule of St. Benedict* (New York: Vintage Books, 1998), p. xv.

p. 60   "Brothers, now that we have asked the Lord": Benedict, *Rule of Life*, pp. 5-6, italics added.

Chapter 5: Mission

p. 65   "Are you looking for purpose in life?": Os Guinness, *The Call* (Nashville: W Publishing, 1998), p. vii.

p. 67   "Discernment at its best is the consequence of a daily": Rueben P. Job, *Guide to Prayer for Spiritual Discernment* (Nashville: Upper Room Books, 1996), p. 82.

p. 69   "Discernment for the Christian community begins with": Ibid., p. 49.

p. 70   his schoolmates called him Virgil: Courtney Anderson, *To the Golden Shore* (Valley Forge, Penn.: Judson Press, 1987), p. 20.

p. 70   Adoniram skipped the freshman coursework: Ibid., p. 31.

p. 70   His friendship with Eames led to the collapse: Ibid., pp. 32-33.

p. 70   "Name was Eames. Jacob Eames": Ibid., p. 44.

p. 70   he feared for his soul: Ibid., p. 46.

pp. 70-71   he skipped the first year of studies: Ibid., p. 48.

p. 71   Judson dedicated himself to God: Ibid., p. 50.

p. 71   "How shall I so order my future being": Ibid.

p. 71   "All at once his imagination kindled": Ibid., p. 53.

p. 71   "during a solitary walk in the woods behind the college": Ibid., p. 57.

p. 71   This is also the day Judson met his first wife: Ibid., pp. 68-70.

p. 71   Adoniram's letter to Deacon John Hasseltine: Ibid., p. 83.

p. 72   By the summer of 1813 they arrived at Rangoon: John Piper, "How Few There Are Who Die So Hard! Suffering and Success in the Life of Adoniram Judson: The Cost of Bringing Christ to Burma," delivered at the Bethlehem Conference for Pastors, Minneapolis, February 4, 2003.

p. 72   "It seems almost too much to believe": Anderson, *Golden Shore*, p. 222.

p. 72   "Adoniram had to write for more tracts": Ibid., pp. 394-95.

p. 72   The missionaries were giving away hundreds of tracts: Ibid., p. 399.

Chapter 6: Time

p. 83   "Most of us feel utterly ransacked": Mark Buchanan, *The Rest of God* (Nashville: Thomas Nelson, 2006).

p. 84   "We mostly spend our lives conjugating three verbs": Evelyn Underhill, *The Spiritual Life* (Harrisburg, Penn.: Morehouse, 1955), p. 20.

p. 88   "True religion, in great part, consists in holy affections": Jonathan Edwards, *Works of Jonathan Edwards*, vol. 2: *Religious Affections*, ed. John E. Smith (New Haven, Conn.: Yale University Press, 2009), p. 95.

p. 88   "It may be inquired, what the affections of the mind are?": Ibid., p. 96.

p. 88   "True religion is evermore a powerful thing": Ibid., p. 100.

p. 88   "The affections are very much the spring of men's actions": Ibid., pp. 100-101.

p. 88   "I am bold to assert, that there never was any considerable change": Ibid., p. 102.

p. 88   "But yet it is evident, that religion consists so much in affection": Ibid., p. 119.

p. 88   Edwards's "Resolutions": See Jonathan Edwards, "Resolutions," The Jonathan Edwards Center at Yale University, http://edwards.yale.edu/archive?path=aHR0cDovL2Vkd2FyZHMueWFsZS5lZHUvY2dpLWJpbi9uZXdwaGlsby9nZXRvYmplY3QucGw/Yy4xNTo3NDoxLndqZW8=.

Chapter 7: Trust

p. 94   *hesed* as "compassionate loyalty": Robert L. Hubbard, *The Book of Ruth*, The New International Commentary on the Old Testament (Grand Rapids: Eerdmans, 1988), p. 1.

p. 94   "exquisitely wrought jewel of Hebrew narrative art": Introduction to Ruth, in *NIV Study Bible* (Grand Rapids: Zondervan), p. 364.

p. 95   kinsman-redeemer: A kinsman-redeemer was a male relative who had the privilege of taking action for a relative who was in trouble, danger or in need of vindication or protection.

p. 95   "No matter how discouraging or antagonistic the world may seem": Introduction to Ruth, *Life Application Bible, NIV* (Wheaton, Ill.: Tyndale House, 1988), p. 421.

p. 95   God is the primary actor in the drama: Edward F. Campbell, *Ruth*, Anchor Yale Bible Commentary 7 (New York: Doubleday, 1975), p. 29.

p. 95   "Ruth's inability to do anything to alter her estate": Introduction to Ruth, *The Spirit-Filled Life Bible, NKJV* (Nashville: Thomas Nelson, 1991), p. 391.

p. 95   goodness exists when we are willing to make the effort: Walter A. Elwell, ed., *Baker's Bible Handbook* (Grand Rapids: Baker), p. 166.

p. 98   secured his spot as a Member of Parliament: John Pollock, *Wilberforce* (New York: St. Martin's Press, 1977), pp. 1-12.

p. 98   "a songster and wit who was professionally careless": Christopher D. Hancock, "The Shrimp Who Stopped Slavery," *Christian History* 17, no. 53 (1997): 14.

p. 98   He was ashamed and tormented by the idea: John Piper, "Reflections on the Life and Labor of William Wilberforce," lecture at Bethlehem Conference for Pastors Baptist Church, Minneapolis, February 5, 2002.

p. 98   "I was filled with sorrow": Pollock, *Wilberforce,* p. 37.

p. 98   "It is hoped and believed that the Lord has raised you up": John Newton, quoted in ibid., p. 38.

p. 99   "God almighty has set before me two great objects": Pollock, *Wilberforce,* p. 69.

p. 99   a bill was passed ensuring that abolition was actually enforced: Hancock, "The Shrimp Who Stopped Slavery," pp. 18-19.

p. 99   Wilberforce and friends founded 220 institutions: Richard V. Pierard, "Little Known Facts About William Wilberforce and the Century of Reform," *Christian History* 17, no. 53 (1997): 3.

p. 99   Tomkins's description of the Clapham Sect: Stephen Tomkins, *The Clapham Sect* (Oxford: Lion UK, 2010), p. 1.

p. 99   "We are thinking of a company of men": John Patten, *These Remarkable Men* (London: Lutterworth, 1945), pp. 11-12.

p. 99   Never a formal organization, the Clapham Sect was: Ibid., p. 13.

p. 99   keenly interested in the new missionary movement: Ibid., p. 14.

p. 100   Wilberforce "routinely gave away a quarter of his income": Stephen Tomkins, *William Wilberforce* (Grand Rapids: Eerdmans, 2007), p. 149.

Chapter 8: Temple

pp. 106-7   "I am fearfully and wonderfully made": John Edmiston, "Our Bodies Are Temples of the Holy Spirit." *GlobalChristians*, www.globalchristians.org/articles/yourbody.htm (accessed November 16, 2010).

p. 109   "the din of scandalous love-affairs raged": Saint Augustine, *The Confessions*, trans. Maria Boulding, from *The Works of Saint Augustine: A Translation for the 21st Century,* ed. John E. Rotelle (New York: New City Press, 1997), p. 75.

p. 110   "Grant me chastity and self-control": Ibid., 8.7.17

p. 110   "so much of him plainly did not belong to this oasis of purity": Ibid., p. 47.

p. 110   Ambrose could defend the Old Testament: Peter Brown, *Augustine of Hippo: A Biography,* (Berkeley: University of California Press, 2000), p. 84.

p. 110   "I flung myself down somehow under a fig-tree": Augustine, *Confessions* 8.12.28.

p. 110   all shades of doubt fled away: Ibid., 8.12.29.

p. 110   "morality of joyless conscientiousness": Henry Chadwick, *Augustine of Hippo: A Life* (Oxford: Oxford University Press, 2009), p. 96.

Chapter 9: Treasure

p. 120   "not in order that we might spend it": George Mueller, *The Autobiography of George Mueller, or A Million and a Half in Answer to Prayer,* comp. G. Fred. Bergin (London: J. Nisbet, 1914), p. 1.

p. 120   "And now at a time when I was as careless": Ibid.

p. 120   Mueller's father was displeased: Ibid., p. 12.

p. 120   Mueller lived in the Orphan House: Ibid., p. 16.

p. 121   Mueller gave up his church salary: Ibid., p. 47.

p. 121   "At the same time it appeared to me right": Ibid.

p. 121   "I had constantly cases brought before me": Ibid., p. 80.

p. 121   First Wilson Street Orphan-House was opened: Ibid., p. 89.

pp. 121-22   "To-day we obtained, without any trouble"; Ibid., p. 92.

p. 122   "In the course of the last seventeen years": Ibid., p. 564.

Chapter 10: Talent

p. 128   Noah built the ark "because a voice had told him to": Frederick Buechner, *Secrets in the Dark* (New York: HarperOne, 2006), p. 46.

p. 129   "When one lives obediently in the center of a call": Gordon MacDonald, "God's Calling Plan," *Leadership Journal* 24 (2003): 42.

p. 130   Fanny's first hymn, "Our Bright Home Above": John Loveland, *Blessed Assurance* (Nashville: Broadman, 1978), p. 100.

p. 130   "My real work as a hymn-writer began from that hour": S. Trevena Jackson, *Fanny Crosby's Story of Ninety-Four Years* (New York: Fleming H. Revell, 1915), p. 64.

p. 130   "How in the world did you manage to write that hymn?": Loveland, *Blessed Assurance*, pp. 102-3.

p. 130   "memorized eight complete books of the Bible": Ibid., p. 128.

p. 130   "Oh must I lose a friendship that I have enjoyed so much?": Ibid., p. 113.

p. 130   "I have sought each day to be one of God's unselfish souls": Jackson, *Fanny Crosby's Story*, p. 173.

p. 131   Fanny was in high demand for speaking engagements: Ibid., p. 196.

p. 131   "The poor doctor, who spoiled my eyes": Loveland, *Blessed Assurance*, pp. 22-23.

pp. 131-32 "Pass Me Not, O Gentle Savior": Fanny J. Crosby (1868).

Chapter 11: Commitment to the Body of Christ

p. 143   covenantal love is the hallmark: See Stephen A. Macchia, *Becoming a Healthy Church* (Grand Rapids: Baker, 2005).

p. 143   "It makes a difference *how one thinks about the church*": Richard C. Halverson, quoted in Jim Peterson, *Church Without Walls* (Colorado Springs: NavPress, 1992), p. 116.

p. 144   "a man of order and peace born into a world of conflict": T. H. L. Parker, *John Calvin: A Biography* (Louisville: Westminster John Knox Press, 2007), p. 9.

p. 144   His father was the notary for the cathedral: Ibid., p. 17.

p. 144   became a clerk for the bishop and received the tonsure: Ibid., p. 20.

p. 144   He most likely needed special permission: Ibid., p. 27.

p. 144   University of Orleans to study law: Ibid., p. 30.

p. 144   Calvin on board with the Reformation: Ibid., p. 19.

p. 144   Cop and Calvin fled to Basel: Ibid., pp. 22-23.

p. 144   "The summit of my wishes was the enjoyment of literary ease": Ibid., p. 24.

p. 144   "we cannot see very far before us": Ibid.

p. 145   "You are simply following your own wishes": Ibid., p. 25.

p. 145   "to realize the idea of the Church that he believed": Ibid., p. 78.

p. 145   "Our true completeness and perfection consist in": John Calvin, *Commentary on Epistle to the Ephesians* (Grand Rapids: Baker, 2003), pp. 281-82.

p. 145   "instructing believers in wholesome doctrine": Parker, *John Calvin*, p. 80.

p. 145   Calvin's primary task was preaching the gospel: Ibid., pp. 80-81.

p. 145   "On Sundays he took always the New Testament": Ibid., p. 82.

p. 145   "Luther and Calvin were no firebrand revolutionaries": Ibid., p. 107.

p. 146   Reformed Churches united by the Consensus of Zurich: Ibid., pp. 114-15.

p. 146   "When he died, all Geneva desired to see his body": Ibid., p. 123.

p. 146   "The church is called 'catholic,' or 'universal' ": John Calvin, *Institutes of the Christian Religion* 4.1.2., trans. Ford Lewis Battles, 2 vols. (Louisville: Westminster John Knox Press, 2006).

p. 146   "For what God has joined together": Ibid., 4.1.1.

p. 146   "The church is referred to as the communion of saints": Ibid., 4.1.3.

p. 146   Community of saints "very well expresses what the church is": Ibid.

pp. 146-47 "If truly convinced that God is the common Father": Ibid.

p. 147   "Wherever we see the Word of God purely preached and heard": Ibid., 4.1.9.

p. 147   "there is nothing that Satan plots more": Ibid., 4.1.11.

p. 147   There is no individual Christianity: Ibid., 4.1.21.

Chapter 12: Context of a Spiritual Community and Friendship
p. 155   "typically met privately in groups of 3 or 4 to pray": Elesha Coffman, "Attack of the Bible-Moths," *Christian History* 20, no. 69 (2001): 20-22.
p. 155   "to cultivate the life of prayer and sacrament": V. H. H. Green, *The Young Mr. Wesley* (New York: St. Martin's, 1961), p. 153.
p. 155   "[He] still sought an ultimate authority and he believed": Ibid., p. 168.
p. 155   "almost a Christian" and "not a whole Christian": Ibid.
pp. 155-156 "the ideal of an apostolic, primitive church": Ibid., p. 286.
p. 156   "He drew from primitive Christianity an ideal": Gwang Seok Oh, *John Wesley's Ecclesiology: A Study in Its Sources and Development,* (Lanham, Md.: Scarecrow Press, 2008), p. 19.
p. 156   class members would give "brief accounts of their religious experience": J. S. Simon, *John Wesley the Master Builder* (London: Epworth Press, 1927), pp. 69-70.
p. 156   If people wanted to officially join a Methodist Society: Ibid., p. 183.
p. 156   "The class meeting, the basic unit of Methodism": Oh, *John Wesley's Ecclesiology,* p. 68.
p. 156   "Class meetings empowered the laity": Ibid., p. 33.
p. 156   Church of England had "failed to bring their members": Ibid., p. 111.
p. 156   Wesley's mother's instructions to him: Ibid., p. 139.
p. 156   "Wesley's practical divinity was accountability in community": Ibid.
p. 156   meeting together in a class meeting was a means of grace: Ibid., p. 179.
p. 156   The list of questions created by John: Charles E. White, "Spare the Rod and Spoil the Church," *Christian History Magazine,* vol. 20, no. 1 (2001): 28-30.
p. 157   "It was openly declared they were not of us": Ibid.
p. 157   "The greatest thing John Wesley ever gave to the world": D. Michael Henderson's *John Wesley's Class Meeting: A Model for Making Disciples* (Nappanee: Ind.: Evangel Publishing, 1997), p. 93.
p. 157   "The servant girl would follow her mistress": Ibid., pp. 99-100.
p. 157   "In this circle of companionship, it was difficult to be evasive": Ibid., p. 102.

Leadership Transformations inc.

Leadership Transformations, Inc. (LTi), was founded in 2003 by Steve and Ruth Macchia for the purpose of fostering spiritual formation, discernment and renewal among Christian leaders and teams. LTi's vision is "for local churches and Christian organizations to be filled with leaders who place spiritual formation and discernment above all other leadership responsibilities." The mission of LTi is "to cultivate vibrant spirituality and attentive discernment among Christian leaders and teams." Our core values include the Trinity, the local church, authentic community, vibrant spirituality and attentive discernment.

LTi focuses on leadership. We believe that a transformed leader means a transformed organization. The greatest transformation comes during times when we quiet ourselves long enough to listen attentively to God, to one another and to what's stirring in our own hearts.

Leadership Transformations seeks to increase the "attentiveness quotient" within individuals and teams—helping them to become more aware of God's presence and direction as he forms them more into the likeness of his son, Jesus, gives them discernment for the path ahead and renews their strength as only he can do. LTi believes that as leaders pursue the deepening of their souls they experience greater vitality in ministry.

The ministry services of LTi include:
- Soul care retreats and soul sabbaths
- Spiritual leadership communities
- Spiritual formation groups
- Spiritual direction
  - Soul care conversations (one-on-one sessions)
  - Selah—certificate program in spiritual direction
- Spiritual discernment for teams
- Spiritual health assessments
  - Church Health Assessment Tool (CHAT)
  - Family Health Assessment (with Focus on the Family)
- Spiritual formation resources
  - Online store (books, reflective readings and retreat resources)
  - Published articles (written by Steve Macchia and other LTi team members)
  - Recommended readings (select bibliography of spiritual formation resources)

For more information on Leadership Transformations visit www.LeadershipTransformations.org or call 877-TEAM LTI (877-832-6584) toll free.

ABOUT THE AUTHOR

Since July 2003, the Rev. Dr. Stephen A. Macchia has served as founder and president of Leadership Transformations, Inc. (www.LeadershipTransformations.org). As a part of his LTi portfolio, he also serves as director of the Pierce Center for Disciple-Building at Gordon-Conwell Theological Seminary, overseeing the center's activities on all four campuses along the east coast (Boston and South Hamilton, Massachusetts, Charlotte North Carolina, and Jacksonville, Florida). He also serves as an instructor in the Doctor of Ministry department at Gordon-Conwell, co-facilitating the track on Spiritual Formation for Ministry Leaders. He previously served as president of Vision New England for fourteen years. Prior to that, he was on the pastoral staff at Grace Chapel, Lexington, Massachusetts, for eleven years. He is the author of several published articles; a devotional guide, *31 Reflections on Discipleship Through the Gospel of John*; and has written five books:

Becoming a Healthy Church (Baker Books, cloth 1999/paper 2003)
Becoming a Healthy Church Workbook (Baker Books, 2001)
Becoming a Healthy Disciple (Baker Books, 2004)
Becoming a Healthy Disciple Small Group Study and Worship Guide (LTi Publications, 2004)
Becoming a Healthy Team (Baker Books, 2005)

He serves as contributing writer for *Church Executive Magazine* and is on the editorial advisory panel for Christianity Today's online weekly publication *BuildingChurchLeaders.com*. He previously served on the executive committee and board of directors of the National Association of Evangelicals. He is also the creator of the online *Church Health Assessment Tool* (CHAT), detailed on www.HealthyChurch.net. The CHAT assessment tool has been taken by over 20,000 individuals in hundreds of churches since its release. LTi recently collaborated with Focus on the Family as developers of their online Family Health Assessment.

Steve Macchia is a leader, teacher, conference speaker, leadership consultant, soul care retreat facilitator, spiritual director, mentor and coach with a passion for inviting committed believers, pastors, leaders and teams into a more intimate walk with the Lord. Steve and his wife, Ruth, live in Massachusetts and are the proud parents of two children, Nathan and Rebekah.

A full bio and photo of Stephen A. Macchia can be viewed at www.LeadershipTransformations.org/macchiabio.htm or www.RuleOfLife.com.

formatio

TRADITION. EXPERIENCE.
TRANSFORMATION.

Formatio books from InterVarsity Press follow the rich tradition of the church in the journey of spiritual formation. These books are not merely about being informed, but about being transformed by Christ and conformed to his image. Formatio stands in InterVarsity Press's evangelical publishing tradition by integrating God's Word with spiritual practice and by prompting readers to move from inward change to outward witness. InterVarsity Press uses the chambered nautilus for Formatio, a symbol of spiritual formation because of its continual spiral journey outward as it moves from its center. We believe that each of us is made with a deep desire to be in God's presence. Formatio books help us to fulfill our deepest desires and to become our true selves in light of God's grace.